Heidegger's Neglect of the Body

SUNY series in Contemporary Continential Philosophy
─────────────
Dennis J. Schmidt, editor

Heidegger's Neglect of the Body

KEVIN A. AHO

Published by
State University of New York Press, Albany

© 2009 State University of New York

For information, contact State University of New York Press, Albany, NY
www.sunypress.edu

Production by Diane Ganeles
Marketing by Michael Campochiaro

Library of Congress Cataloging-in-Publication Data

Aho, Kevin, 1969-
  Heidegger's neglect of the body / Kevin A. Aho.
     p. cm.
  Includes bibliographical references and index.
  ISBN 978-1-4384-2775-1 (hardcover : alk. paper)
  1. Heidegger, Martin, 1889–1976.   2. Body, Human (Philosophy)
I. Title.

  B3279.H49A39 2009
  128'.6092—dc22   2008050717

10 9 8 7 6 5 4 3 2 1

For Charles Guignon

Contents

Acknowledgments

This project would not have been completed without the loving support of my beautiful wife, Elena. She, my parents, Jim and Margaret Aho, and my brothers, Ken and Kyle, have been a continual source of strength, inspiration, and joy. To my teachers at the University of South Florida, where this project was originally conceived, I am thankful to Stephen Turner, Ofelia Schutte, and Joanne Waugh. For their careful reading and recommendations, I am thankful to Hans Pedersen and Bill Koch. I am also deeply appreciative of my supportive colleagues at Florida Gulf Coast University, especially Sean Kelly, Kim Jackson, Glenn Whitehouse, Maria Roca, Jim Wohlpart, Karen Tolchin, and Tom Demarchi. Most of all, I am indebted to my teacher and dear friend, Charles Guignon. His intellectual guidance, encouragement, and wonderful sense of humor over the years kept this project going. His friendship has been a gift in my life, and this book is dedicated to him.

I would also like to thank the editors and publishers of the following journals for permission to reprint portions of the following articles:

"Metontology and the Body-Problem in *Being and Time*." *Auslegung* 28:2 (2006): 1–20. Peter Montecuollo, ed. (ch. 1).

"The Missing Dialogue between Heidegger and Merleau-Ponty: On the Importance of the Zollikon Seminars." *Body and Society* 11:2 (2005): 1–2. Mike Featherstone and Bryan Turner, eds. (ch. 2).

"Gender and Time: Revisiting the Question of Dasein's Neutrality." *Epoché* 12:1 (2007): 137–155. Walter Brogan, ed. (ch. 3).

"Animality Revisited: The Question of Life in Heidegger's Early Freiburg Lectures." *Existentia* 16: 5–6 (2006): 379–392. Gábor Ferge, ed. (ch. 4).

"Logos and the Poverty of Animals: Rethinking Heidegger's Humanism." *The New Yearbook for Phenomenology and Phenomenological*

Philosophy 7 (2007): 109–126. Steven Crowell and Burt Hopkins, eds. (ch. 4).

"Simmel on Acceleration, Boredom, and Extreme Aesthesia." *Journal for the Theory of Social Behavior* 37:4 (2007): 447–462. Charles Smith, ed. (ch. 5).

"Acceleration and Time Pathologies: The Critique of Psychology in Heidegger's Beiträge." *Time and Society* 16:1 (2007): 25–42. Robert Hassan, ed. (ch. 5).

"Recovering Play: On the Relationship between Leisure and Authenticity in Heidegger's Thought." *Janus Head* 10:1 (2007): 217–238. Brent Robbins, ed. (ch. 6).

For permission to reprint a selection from Thich Nhat Hanh I am grateful to Parallax Press for the excerpt from *The Heart of Understanding: Commentaries on the Prajñaparamita Heart Sutra*, by Thich Nhat Hanh (Berkeley, CA: Parallax Press, 1988), www.parallax.org.

Abbreviations

Works by Heidegger

"GA" indicates the volume of the *Gesamtausgabe* (*Collected Works*). Frankfurt am Main: Vittorio Klostermann. The lecture/publication date follows the German title. Unless otherwise indicated, all references are from the English translation and pagination.

AWP   *Die Zeit des Weltbildes*. 1938. (GA 5). "The Age of the World Picture." In *The Question Concerning Technology and Other Essays*, trans. William Lovitt. New York: Harper and Row, 1977.

BDT   *Bauen Wohnen Denken*. 1951. (GA 7). "Building Dwelling Thinking." In *Basic Writings*, trans. Albert Hofstadter. New York: HarperCollins, 1993.

BP   *Die Grundprobleme der Phänomenologie*. 1927. (GA 24). *The Basic Problems of Phenomenology*. Translated by Albert Hofstadter. Bloomington: Indiana University Press, 1982.

BQP   *Grundfragen der Philosophie: Ausgewählte "Probleme" der "Logik."* 1937. (GA 45). *Basic Questions of Philosophy: Selected "Problems" of "Logic."* Translated by Richard Rojcewicz and André Shuwer. Bloomington: Indiana University Press, 1994.

BT   *Sein und Zeit*. 1927. (GA 2). *Being and Time*. Translated by John Macquarrie and Edward Robinson. New York: Harper and Row, 1978.

CP   *Beiträge zur Philosophie (Vom Ereignis)*. 1936–1938. (GA 65). *Contributions to Philosophy (From Enowning)*. Translated by Parvis Emad and Kenneth Maly. Bloomington: Indiana University Press, 1999.

CT   *Der Begriff der Zeit*. 1924. (GA 64). *The Concept of Time*. Translated by William McNeill. Oxford: Blackwell, 1992.

DHW   *Wilhelm Diltheys Forschungsarbeit und der Kampf um eine historische Weltanschauung*. 1925. (GA 80). "Wilhelm Dilthey's Research and the Struggle for a Historical Worldview." In *Supplements: From the Earliest Essays to* Being and Time *and Beyond*, trans. Charles Bambach. Albany: State University of New York Press, 2002.

DT   *Gelassenheit*. 1955. (GA 16). "Memorial Address." In *Discourse on Thinking*, trans. John Anderson and E. Hans Freund. New York: Harper and Row, 1966.

ET   *Vom Wesen der Wahrheit*. 1930. (GA 9). "On the Essence of Truth." In *Basic Writing*, trans. John Sallis. New York: HarperCollins, 1993.

FCM   *Die Grundbegriffe der Metaphysik: Welt, Endlichkeit, Einsamkeit*. 1929–1930. (GA 29/30). *Fundamental Concepts of Metaphysics: World, Finitude, Solitude*. Translated by William McNeill and Nicholas Walker. Bloomington: Indiana University Press, 1995.

FS   *Seminare—Zähringen*. 1973. (GA 15). "Seminar in Zähringen." In *Four Seminars*, trans. Andrew Mitchell and François Raffoul. Bloomington: Indiana University Press, 2003.

HCT   *Prolegomena zur Geschichte des Zeitbegriffs*. 1925. (GA 20). *History of the Concept of Time: Prolegomena*. Translated by Theodore Kisiel. Bloomington: Indiana University Press, 1985.

HF   *Ontologie: Hermeneutik der Faktizität*. 1923. (GA 63). *Ontology: The Hermeneutics of Facticity*. Translated by John van Buren. Bloomington: Indiana University Press, 1999.

HS   *Seminare—Heraklit*. 1966–1967. (GA 15). *Heraclitus Seminar, 1966/67* (with Eugen Fink). Translated by Charles H. Seibert. Evanston, IL: Northwestern University Press, 1993.

IM   *Einführung in die Metaphysik*. 1935. (GA 40). *Introduction to Metaphysics*. Translated by Gregory Fried and Richard Polt. New Haven, CT: Yale University Press, 2000.

IP   *Einleitung in die Philosophy*. 1928–1929. (GA 27). *Introduction to Philosophy*. Translation in preparation. References are from the German pagination. Frankfurt am Main: Vittorio Klostermann, 1996.

KPM   *Kant und das Problem der Metaphysik*. 1929. (GA 3). *Kant and the Problem of Metaphysics*. Translated by Richard Taft. Bloomington: Indiana University Press, 1997.

LA   *Die Sprache*. 1950. (GA 12). "Language." In *Poetry, Language, Thought,* trans. Albert Hofstadter. New York: Harper and Row, 1971.

LH   *Brief über den Humanismus*. 1947. (GA 9). "Letter on Humanism." In *Basic Writings*, trans. Frank Capuzzi and J. Glenn Gray. New York: HarperCollins 1993.

LS   *Logos (Heraklit, Fragment 50)*. 1951. (GA 7). "Logos (Heraclitus, Fragment B 50)." In *Early Greek Thinking*, trans. David F. Krell and Frank A. Capuzzi. New York: Harper and Row, 1975.

MFL   *Metaphysische Anfangsgründe der Logik im Ausgang von Leibniz*. 1928. (GA 26). *Metaphysical Foundations of Logic*. Translated by Michael Heim. Bloomington: Indiana University Press, 1984.

N1   *Der Wille zur Macht als Kunst*. 1936–1937. (GA 6). "The Will to Power as Art." In *Nietzsche Vol. 1*, trans. David F. Krell. New York: Harper and Row, 1979.

N2   *Die ewige Wiederkehr des Gleichen*. 1937. (GA 6). "The Eternal Recurrence of the Same." In *Nietzsche Vol. II*, trans. David F. Krell. New York: Harper and Row, 1984.

N3   *Der Wille zur Macht als Erkenntnis*. 1939. (GA 6). "The Will to Power as Knowledge and as Metaphysics." In *Nietzsche Vol. III*, trans. Joan Stambaugh, David F. Krell, and Frank A. Capuzzi. New York: Harper and Row, 1984.

N4   *Der europäische Nihilismus*. 1940. (GA 6). "European Nihilism." In *Nietzsche Vol. IV*, trans. Frank A. Capuzzi. New York: Harper and Row, 1982.

NL   *Das Wesen der Sprache*. 1957. (GA 12). "The Nature of Language." In *On the Way to Language*, trans. Peter D. Hertz. New York: Harper and Row, 1971.

OH   *Hölderlins Hymnen "Wie wenn am Feiertage ..."* 1941. (GA 4). "Hölderlin's Hymn 'As When On Holiday ...' " In *Elucidations of Hölderlin's Poetry*, trans. Keith Hoeller. Amherst, NY: Humanity Books, 2000.

OTB   *Zeit und Sein*. 1962. (GA 14). *On Time and Being*. Translated by Joan Stambaugh. New York: Harper and Row, 1972.

OWA   *Der Ursprung des Kunstwerkes*. 1935. (GA 5). "The Origin of the Work of Art." In *Basic Writings*, trans. Albert Hofstadter. New York: HarperCollins, 1993.

PA   *Phänomenologische Interpretationen zu Aristoteles: Einführung in die phänomenologische Forschung.* 1921. (GA 61). *Phenomenological Interpretations of Aristotle: Initiation into Phenomenological Research.* Translated by Richard Rojcewicz. Bloomington: Indiana University Press, 2001.

PS   *Platon: Sophistes.* 1924–1925. (GA 19). *Plato's Sophist.* Translated by Richard Rojcewicz and André Schuwer. Bloomington: Indiana University Press, 2003.

QCT   *Die Frage nach der Technik.* 1949. (GA 7). "The Question Concerning Technology." In *The Question Concerning Technology and Other Essays*, trans. William Lovitt. New York: Harper and Row, 1977.

RE   *Hölderlins Hymnen "Andenken."* 1943. (GA 4). "Hölderlin's Hymn 'Remembrance.' " In *Elucidations of Hölderlin's Poetry*, trans. Keith Holler. Amherst, NY: Humanity Books, 2000.

TDP   *Zur Bestimmung der Philosophie.* 1919. (GA 56/57). *Towards the Definition of Philosophy.* Translated by Ted Sadler. London: Continuum Books, 2002.

TT   *Das Ding.* 1951. (GA 7). "The Thing." In *Poetry, Language, Thought*, trans. Albert Hofstadter. New York: Harper and Row, 1971.

TU   *Die Kehre.* 1949. (GA 79). "The Turning." In *The Question Concerning Technology and Other Essays*, trans. William Lovitt. New York: Harper and Row, 1977.

WCT   *Was heisst Denken?* 1951–1952. (GA 8). *What Is Called Thinking?* Translated by J. Glenn Gray. New York: Harper and Row, 1968.

WIT   *Die Frage nach dem Ding.* 1935. (GA 41). *What Is a Thing?* Translated by W. B. Barton and Vera Deutsch. South Bend, IN: Regenery/Gateway, 1967.

WL   *Der Weg zur Sprache.* 1959. (GA 12). "The Way of Language." In *On the Way to Language*, trans. Peter D. Hertz. New York: HarperCollins, 1971.

ZS   *Zollikoner Seminare. 1959–1972.* (GA 89). *Zollikon Seminars.* Translated by Franz Mayr and Richard Askey. Evanston, IL: Northwestern University Press, 2001.

Works by Jacques Derrida

G1   *"Geschlecht*: Sexual Difference, Ontological Difference." In
      Feminist Interpretations of Martin Heidegger, ed. Nancy J. Hol-
      land and Patricia Huntington. University Park: Pennsylvania
      State University Press, 2001.

G2   *"Geschlecht* II: Heidegger's Hand." In *Deconstruction and Phi-
      losophy: The Texts of Jacques Derrida*, ed. John Sallis, trans. John
      P. Leavey Jr. Chicago, IL: University of Chicago Press, 1987.

MP   *Margins of Philosophy*. Translated by Alan Bass. Chicago, IL:
      University of Chicago Press, 1982.

OS   *Of Spirit: Heidegger and the Question*. Translated by Geoffrey
      Bennington and Rachel Bowlby. Chicago, IL: University of
      Chicago Press, 1989.

Works by Luce Irigaray

JTN   *je, tu, nous: Toward a Culture of Difference*. Translated by Alison
      Martin. New York: Routledge Press, 1993.

SG   *Sexes and Geneologies*. Translated by Gillian C. Gill. New York:
      Columbia University Press, 1993.

SWN   *The Sex Which Is Not One*. Translated by Gillian C. Gill. Ithaca,
      NY: Cornell University Press, 1985.

Works by Maurice Merleau-Ponty

PP   *Phenomenology of Perception*. Translated by Colin Smith. New
      York: Routledge, 1962.

VI   *The Visible and the Invisible, Followed by Working Notes*. Translated
      by Alphonso Lingis. Evanston, IL: Northwestern University
      Press, 1968.

Introduction

The Body Problem

It has been over fifty years since French philosophers began criticizing the "starting-point" (*Ausgang*) of *Being and Time* (1927)—specifically Heidegger's account of everyday practices, practices that initially give us "access" (*Zugang*) to the question of the meaning of being. Alphonse de Waelhens, for example, argued that Heidegger's phenomenology completely overlooks the fundamental role played by perception in particular and the body in general in our everyday understanding of things. "[In] *Being and Time*," says Waelhens, "one does not find thirty lines concerning the problem of perception; one does not find ten concerning that of the body."[1] Jean-Paul Sartre amplified this line of criticism when he emphasized the importance of the body as the first point of contact that a human being has with its world, a contact that is prior to detached theorizing about objects.

Of the early French phenomenologists, Maurice Merleau-Ponty's work has been the most influential. He laid the foundations for a critique of Heidegger through his systematic analysis of the primacy of bodily perception, particularly in terms of our spatial directionality and orientation, a sensual orientation that makes it possible for us to handle worldly equipment in the first place.[2] Merleau-Ponty's account of embodiment has since been developed and refined by English-speaking commentators such as Hubert Dreyfus, David Cerbone, and David Krell.[3] Krell formulates the problem this way:

> Did Heidegger simply fail to see the arm of the everyday body rising in order to hammer the shingles onto the roof, did he overlook the quotidian gaze directed toward the ticking watch that overtakes both sun and moon, did he miss the body poised daily in its brazen car, a car equipped with a turn signal fabricated by and for the hand and eye

1

of man, did he neglect the human being capable day-in and day-out of moving its body and setting itself in motion? If so, what conclusion must we draw?[4]

In *Being and Time* there is little acknowledgment of the "lived-body" (*Leib*) that prereflectively negotiates its way through the world, a body that is already spatially oriented in terms of directionality as it reaches out and faces the various tools and others that are encountered every day.[5] Heidegger merely offers this remark:

> Dasein's spatialization in its "bodily nature" is likewise marked out in accordance with these directions. [This "bodily nature" hides a whole problematic of its own, though we shall not treat it here.] (BT, 143)

This Merleau-Pontyian criticism has been recently fortified by feminist critics following the 1983 publication of Jacques Derrida's essay "*Geschlecht*: Sexual Difference, Ontological Difference." His essay helped pave the way for two decades of commentary, which attempts to enrich Heidegger's project by addressing the possibility of a gendered incarnation of human existence (*Dasein*). For Heidegger—specifically in his 1928 Marburg lectures on Leibniz—Dasein is regarded as "neutral" (*neutrale*) or "asexual" (*geschlechtslos*) insofar as it exists prior to and makes possible an understanding of sexed bodies and gendered practices. This position has left many feminist commentators dissatisfied. If one of the goals of Heidegger's early project is to recover concrete, embodied ways of being, ways of being that are more original than disembodied theorizing, then Heidegger would do well to acknowledge the ways in which these concrete practices are shaped and guided by sexual difference. By giving an account of Dasein's gendered incarnation, Heidegger's analysis of human existence would have recognized the social hierarchies and oppressive relations that already exist in our everyday dealings. This recognition would have allowed for a more complete picture of the way in which human beings dwell in an understanding of being.

In addition to these feminist criticisms, there has been a recent explosion of commentary in the secondary literature that addresses Heidegger's account of the relationship between humans and animals, particularly in his 1929–1930 Freiburg lecture course "The Fundamental Concepts of Metaphysics."[6] In these lectures, Heidegger appears to perpetuate the oppositional prejudices of traditional humanism by arguing that there is a fundamental difference between animal "behavior" (*Benehmen*) and human "comportment" (*Verhalten*). This difference, according to Heidegger, leaves nature in the domain of "unmeaning" (*unsinniges*) and animals without an understanding of being. As a result, animals are regarded as impoverished or "poor in world" (*weltarm*), while human practices are always meaningful and "world-forming (*welt-bildend*). A number of critics have argued that Heidegger's conception of Dasein needs to be expanded to include the body that is organically connected to nature and to the most primitive forms of life. Based on this view, our embodied interconnectedness to animals is regarded as fundamental to the way we make sense of things.

What these criticisms tend to suggest is that Heidegger's project is missing an explicit recognition of how the body participates in shaping our everyday understanding of things. Indeed, if one of Heidegger's core motivations is to reveal how beings "always already" (*immer schon*) make sense to us in the course of everyday life, then it appears that the body should be interpreted as—in the language of *Being and Time*—an "existentiale" (*Existenzial*), an essential structure or condition for any instance of Dasein. David Cerbone explains, "The body would seem to be immediately implicated in [Heidegger's] phenomenology of everyday activity. . . . For this activity involves the manipulation of concrete items such as hammers, pens, doorknobs, and the like, and those manipulations are effected by means of the body."[7] While acknowledging the merits of these criticisms, the goal of this book is to address the question of *why* Heidegger may have bypassed an analysis of the body in the first place and *where* such an analysis might fit within the overall context of his project.

In the following, I suggest that the criticisms of Heidegger regarding his neglect of the body hinge largely on a misinterpretation of Heidegger's use of the word "Dasein." For Heidegger, Dasein is not to be understood in terms of everyday human existence or embodied agency but—from his earliest Freiburg lectures onward—as an unfolding historical horizon or space of meaning that is already "there" (*Da*), prior to the emergence of the human body and its various capacities. Heidegger reminds us of this point thirty years after the publication of *Being and Time* in his seminars in Zollikon:

> The *Da* in *Being and Time* does not mean a statement of place for a being, but rather it should designate the openness where beings can be present for the human being, and the human being also for himself. The *Da* of [Dasein's] being distinguishes the humanness of the human being. (ZS, 120)

I argue that it is only on the basis of an already opened horizon of meaning that we can understand and make sense of beings in the first place, including the "corporeal body" (*Körper*), the "lived-body" (*Leib*), and all of its manifestations. This, however, does not mean that Heidegger dismisses the value of phenomenological investigations of the body, but that such investigations are not crucial to his program of "fundamental ontology." Indeed, in *Being and Time*, Heidegger proposes that the phenomena of the "body," "life," and "consciousness" are all areas of regional inquiry that are worthy of phenomenological investigation in their own right, but such investigations are rendered intelligible only *on the basis of* Dasein (BT, 143, 75, 151). In this regard, fundamental ontology—understood as the inquiry into the meaning of being in general—is more original than any analysis of the body.

Before moving on, it is important to acknowledge that Heidegger appeared to be genuinely troubled by his own inability to address the body problem, particularly in his early writings. Although Heidegger recognized the importance of the spatial directionality of the body in *Being and Time* and continued to engage the problem of embodiment in his 1929–1930 lectures on animals and biology, in his Nietzsche lectures of 1936–1937, in his 1947 "Letter on Humanism," and especially in his decade-long seminars in Zollikon from 1959 to 1971, toward the end of his career he began to recognize that the topic of embodiment presented special difficulties that he was simply not equipped to deal with. In his Heraclitus seminars of 1966–1967, he referred to the body as "the most difficult problem" (HS, 147), and in 1972 he makes his most revealing remark, admitting that he was unable to respond to earlier French criticism regarding the neglect of the body in *Being and Time*, because "the bodily [*das Leibliche*] is the most difficult [problem to understand] and I was unable to say more at the time" (ZS, 231).

Chapter Overview

Chapter 1, "Heidegger's Project," offers a brief introduction to Heidegger's early project, introduces core concepts that will be revisited throughout this book, and identifies themes that reveal a consistency and cohesion to Heidegger's thought throughout his career. Chapters 2, 3, and 4 address the core criticisms of the body problem in the secondary Heidegger literature. Chapter 2, "The Missing Dialogue between Heidegger and Merleau-Ponty," offers an account of the Merleau-Pontyian criticism and provides a detailed analysis of

Heidegger's Zollikon seminars, which explicitly engage the body problem in a way that overlaps significantly with the phenomenology of Merleau-Ponty. Chapter 3, "Gender and Time: On the Question of Dasein's Neutrality," addresses recent feminist criticisms that challenge Heidegger's claim of Dasein's sexual neutrality by indicating the ways in which our everyday understanding of things is already colored by sexual difference. Chapter 4, "Life, Logos, and the Poverty of Animals," addresses the work of a growing number of critics who have questioned Heidegger for downplaying our bodily kinship with animals, portraying animals as impoverished, or "world-poor," and humans as "world-forming."

After situating the body problem within the context of Heidegger's overall project, I hope to show that Heidegger—though rarely discussing the body itself—nonetheless makes a significant contribution to theories of embodiment. This is evident not only in his familiar discussions of our engagement with "handy" (*zuhanden*) tools but especially in his groundbreaking analysis of moods, most notably the pervasive cultural affects of anxiety and boredom that are symptomatic of modern life. In light of these contributions, chapter 5, "The Accelerated Body," examines Heidegger's notion of "acceleration" (*Beschleunigung*), introduced in his *Contributions to Philosophy* (1936–1938), as one of the three symptoms—along with "calculation" and the "outbreak of massiveness"—that characterizes our technological existence. In this chapter, I unpack the relationship between these symptoms and explore the ways in which they form and de-form the body. By supplementing Heidegger's insights with recent findings in social psychology, I suggest that the body is becoming increasingly fragmented and emotionally overwhelmed from chronic sensory arousal and time pressure. This experience not only damages the body physiologically, but it makes it increasingly difficult to qualitatively distinguish what matters to us in our everyday lives, resulting in what Heidegger calls "deep boredom" (*tiefe Langeweile*) (FCM, 134).

Chapter 6, "Recovering Play: On Authenticity and Dwelling," expands on the problem of the accelerated body by attempting to reconcile two conflicting accounts of authenticity in Heidegger's thought. Authenticity in *Being and Time* is commonly interpreted in "existentialist" terms as willful commitment and "resoluteness" (*Entschlossenheit*) in the face of one's own death, but by the late 1930s, it is reintroduced, in terms of *Gelassenheit*, as a nonwillful openness that "lets beings be." By employing Heidegger's conception of authentic "historicality" (*Geschichtlichkeit*), understood as the retrieval of Dasein's past, I suggest that the ancient interpretation of leisure and festivity may play an important role in unifying these conflicting accounts. Genuine leisure, interpreted as a form of "play" (*Spiel*), frees us from technological busy-ness and gives us an opening to face the abyssal nature of our own being and the mystery that "beings are" in the first place. To this end, leisure reconnects us to the original Greek temperament of "wonder" (*Erstaunen*), an embodied disposition that does not seek accelerated mastery and control over beings but calmly accepts the unsettledness of being and is, as a result, allowed into the original openness or play of "time-space" (*Zeit-Raum*) that lets beings emerge-into-presence on their own terms.

Although it critically engages the various manifestations of the body problem in the secondary literature and offers ways to fruitfully appropriate a theory of embodiment from Heidegger, the central aim of this book is to show that Heidegger was not, at bottom, interested in giving an account of embodied agency. It is true that he begins his analytic of Dasein with descriptions of concrete, practical activity, but these descriptions are important only insofar as they "point to" or "indicate" (*anzeigen*) structures that open up a space or "clearing" (*Lichtung*) of meaning, which makes possible any interpretation or understanding of beings. Thus the core motivation of Heidegger's project is not to offer phenomenological investigations into everyday life but to inquire into the meaning of being itself. And this inquiry ultimately leads us beyond the question of embodied agency to the structures of meaning itself. For Heidegger, it is only on the basis of these structures that we can begin to make sense of things—such as bodies—in the first place.

1

Heidegger's Project

In his 1935 summer semester lecture course at the University of Freiburg, entitled "Introduction to Metaphysics," Heidegger asks a seemingly innocuous question: "How does it stand with being?," or, translated in a colloquial sense: "How's it going with being?" (IM, 41)[1] The answer is: not well. Today, humankind is consumed by an instrumental relationship with beings; we have closed off other world-views, forcing all beings—including humans—to show up or reveal themselves in only one way, as objects to be efficiently manipulated and controlled. The prognosis, according to Heidegger, is bleak. In an oft-quoted passage from these lectures, he gives his assessment:

> The spiritual decline of the earth has progressed so far that people are in danger of losing their last spiritual strength, the strength that makes it possible even to see the decline and to appraise it as such. This simple observation has nothing to do with cultural pessimism—nor with any optimism either, of course; for the darkening of the world, the flight of the gods, the destruction of the earth, the reduction of human beings into a mass, the hatred and mistrust of everything creative and free has already reached such proportions throughout the whole earth that such childish categories as pessimism and optimism have become laughable. (IM, 40–41)

Heidegger refers to this modern predicament as "nihilism." Nihilism shows itself when the "question of being" (*Seinsfrage*) is forgotten and humankind is concerned with the world only as a vast storehouse of beings to be used. Nihilism, on this view, is the "spiritual decline of the earth," where human beings "have long since fallen out of being, without knowing it" (IM, 39). The culprit for this spiritual decline is the metaphysical worldview itself.

Heidegger contends that the history of Western philosophy, beginning with Plato and Aristotle, has failed to carry out the proper task of thinking. Philosophy has occupied itself only with beings. It has, therefore, failed to ask the "question of being," a question that asks *how* and *why* beings show up *as* they do. One of the fundamental goals of Heidegger's project, in this regard, is to dismantle a core assumption in the Western philosophical tradition, an assumption that Jacques Derrida will later call the "metaphysics of presence"[2] and Dorothea Frede will call "substance ontology."[3] The history of metaphysics, as Heidegger puts it, is

> the treatment of the meaning of being as *parousia* or *ousia*, which signifies in ontologico-Temporal terms, "presence" (*Anwesenheit*). Entities are grasped in their being as "presence," that is to say, they are understood with regard to a definite mode of time—the *"Present"* (*Gegenwart*). (BT, 47)

Based on this view, the being of anything that exists, including humans, must be understood in terms of enduring presence, a presence that is constant or remains the same through any change in properties. The metaphysical tradition, therefore, understands the being of beings as "substance," referring to the basic, underlying "what-ness" that is unchangeable and essential to all beings as beings.[4] In short, metaphysics is a type of reflection that is "concerned with the essence of *what is*" (AWP, 115). Throughout Western history, this metaphysical assumption prevailed, where substance has been interpreted in different epochs in terms of *eidos* (Plato), *energeia* (Aristotle), *ens creatum* by God (Christendom), *res cogitans/res extensa* (Descartes), and, today, as a material resource, a "standing reserve" (*Bestand*) that can be mastered and controlled by calculative reason (OWA, 201).

As an area of philosophical inquiry, Heidegger sees nothing inherently wrong with metaphysics. The problem is that the metaphysical worldview has become so dominant that it "drives out every other possibility of revealing" (QCT, 27). Consequently, the metaphysical worldview becomes absolute; it fails to recognize that it is merely one of many possible interpretations of the world. Although metaphysics is the prevailing historical interpretation, it has become tyrannical in the modern age, preventing any other possible horizon of disclosure. According to Heidegger, this concealment of other modes of disclosure is a "double-concealment." First, metaphysics forces all things to be contained within a substance-oriented worldview. Second, metaphysics offers itself as the only possible worldview. As a consequence, beings reveal themselves only in terms of substance, and this orientation culminates in the technological age, where our relation with the world has become purely instrumental, where beings show up exclusively as resources at our disposal. But the expansion of the metaphysical worldview does not end with the Cartesian paradigm of man as subject mastering and controlling objects in the world. Man too is sucked into the vast system of objects via the totalizing effects of modern technology. Heidegger asks, "Does not man himself belong even more originally than nature within the standing reserve?" The answer is *yes*, as a "human resource" (QCT, 18).

Dismantling Cartesian Metaphysics

Heidegger's diagnosis of the oblivion of being helps us understand his motivation for overcoming the subject/object metaphysics that "pervades all the problems of modern philosophy" (BP, 124). For Heidegger, this requires engaging the thought of René Descartes, the progenitor of this bifurcated worldview. Descartes's project was to systematically doubt the veracity of every thought and every commonsense experience in order to ground science on a foundation of absolute certainty. This method of radical doubt establishes the *res cogitans* as indubitable. The free, thinking "subject" becomes the self-enclosed first ground from which "objects" of experience can be observed. From this standpoint, the external world comes to be understood as a system of causally determined parts. Beings are no longer experienced in terms of historically embedded social meanings and values but in terms of brute, mechanistic causal relations that can be objectively researched, measured, and predicted based on scientific principles.

Heidegger was particularly troubled by Descartes's project, because it regarded humans as essentially free "individuals," as self-contained subjects with no roots to a shared, historical lifeworld. Modern man becomes the disengaged master of all things. As a consequence, the world shows up in only one way—as a storehouse of objects waiting to be manipulated by the subject. Max Weber warned of the dangers of this Cartesian worldview in his 1918 speech "Science as a Vocation" by challenging Germany's growing commitment to instrumental reason. For Weber, this "increasing intellectualization and rationalization . . . means that there are no more mysterious incalculable forces that come into play, but rather that one can, in principle, master all things by calculation. This means that the world is *disenchanted*."[5] Weber claims that scientific "progress" has no meaning beyond the

"purely practical and technical." Scientific progress is endless and ultimately meaningless in terms of the existential questions that are most
important: "What shall we do and how shall we live?" "How shall
we arrange our lives?" "What is the meaning of our own death?"[6] In
the modern age, life and death have no meaning. Weber writes:

> [They have] none because the individual life of civilized
> man, placed in an infinite "progress," according to its own
> imminent meaning, should never come to an end; for there is
> always a further step ahead of one who stands in the march
> of progress. . . . Because death is meaningless, civilized life
> as such is meaningless; by its very "progressiveness" it
> gives death the imprint of meaninglessness.[7]

Heidegger agrees with Weber's assessment of modern civilization as a disenchanted "iron cage." Scientific progress, interpreted in
terms of instrumental mastery of all things, has stripped the mystery,
the existential meaning and value, from life and has forgotten death
as the "ultimate instance" of life. Yet Heidegger wants to go farther
than Weber. He seeks to "de-structure" the modern understanding of
being itself in order to uncover its origins and recover a more original,
authentic understanding of being that has been distorted and concealed
by our current objectifying tradition.

Heidegger begins his de-structuring of the history of metaphysics
by questioning the traditional interpretation of human being, which
has long been regarded as *a* being: "a rational animal, an *ego cogito*, a
subject, the 'I,' spirit, person, [and so forth]." "But these [beings],' says
Heidegger, "remain uninterrogated as to their being and its structure,
in accordance with the thoroughgoing way in which the question of
being has been neglected" (BT, 44). What is neglected in traditional
metaphysics is an inquiry into human existence itself, into the being
of human beings. In his 1927 Marburg lectures, "The Basic Problems
of Phenomenology," Heidegger suggests that Cartesian metaphysics
presupposes this existential inquiry and for this reason "continues to
work with the ancient metaphysical problems and thus, along with
everything new, still remains within the tradition" (BP, 124). Modern
philosophy, in this regard, fails to ask: What is the unique *way of
being* of the subject?

> It will be expected that ontology now takes the subject as
> the exemplary entity and interprets the concept of being by
> looking at the mode of being of the subject—that henceforth

the subject's *way of being* becomes an ontological problem. But this is precisely what does not happen. (BP, 123)

Heidegger clarifies this point in *Being and Time* when he writes:

> With the cogito sum Descartes claims to prepare a new and secure foundation for philosophy. But what he leaves undetermined in this "radical" beginning is the manner of being of the *res cogitans*, more precisely, the meaning of being of the "sum." (BT, 46)

Heidegger attempts to retrieve the forgotten question of being by investigating that being that is already concerned for its being, namely, humans. Heidegger insists that, prior to any theoretical speculation about beings, we exist, a concerned existence that makes it possible to theorize in the first place. "The existential nature of man," says Heidegger, "is the reason why man can represent beings as such, and why he can be conscious of them. All consciousness presupposes . . . existence as the essential of man."[8] In the course of our workaday lives, we already embody a tacit concern for things, and this concern is mediated by a particular sociohistorical context. Thus Heidegger turns his attention to a way of being more primordial than detached theorizing, which is disclosed in our average everyday practices, our "being-in-the-world" (*In-der-Welt-sein*).

Dasein and Everydayness

Heidegger employs the method of "phenomenology" in order to give an account of our everyday way of being. Phenomenology attempts to describe how things initially show themselves immediately and directly in the course of our "lived-experience" (*Er-lebnis*). This self-showing is pretheoretical or "originary," thus the discoveries of phenomenology are prior to the objective properties and characteristics that are imposed on things by scientific theories or commonsense assumptions. Because it is an original return to the self-showing of things, phenomenology is essentially distinct from the other sciences in that it is not an explanatory "proof." "It says nothing about the material content of the thematic object of science, but speaks only . . . of *how*, the way in which something is" (HCT, 85). Phenomenology, in this regard, is not an explanation; rather, it signifies a method that describes the way human beings encounter things "proximally and for the most part," as they are revealed in everyday, concrete situations. Employing the phenomenological method, Heidegger begins by describing his own "average everyday" involvements. He explains:

> We must choose such a way of access and such a kind of interpretation that this entity can show itself in itself and from itself [*an ihm selbst von ihm selbst her*]. And this means that it is to be shown as it is *proximally and for the most part*—in its *average everydayness.* (BT, 37–38)

By examining his own "factical" life in this manner, Heidegger discovers that he is "always already" (*immer schon*) involved in the question of being in a specific, concrete way. On Heidegger's view, being is always already an issue for me, and I embody a unique understanding of being in the context of my everyday practices. Hence, the question of being starts with an inquiry into my own particular understanding of being, what Heidegger calls "existentiell" (*existenziell*) understanding. "The question of existence never gets straightened out except through existing itself. The understanding of oneself which leads along this way we call *existentiell*" (BT, 33). Heidegger identifies this phenomenological starting point early on in his career. For instance, in 1921 he writes:

> I work concretely and factically from my "I am"—from my spiritual and overall factical origin—milieu—contexts of life—and from that which is accessible to me as living experience—wherein I live—this facticity, as existentiell, is no mere blind Dasein—it lies therewith in existence—that means, however that I live—this "I must" of which one talks—with this facticity of Being-so.[9]

The *existentiell* inquiry into my own particular understanding of being is to be distinguished from Heidegger's fundamental aim, namely, the "existential" (*existenzial*) inquiry into the essential structures (*Existentialia*) of any understanding of being whatsoever. I will return to this distinction later, but first we must give a more detailed account of what Heidegger means by human being (*Dasein*).

Heidegger departs from the metaphysical tradition by referring to human being not in terms of *a* being, a spirit, a subject, or material body but as Dasein, a unique self-interpreting, self-understanding *way of being*. In this regard, Heidegger is not concerned with the objective "what-ness" of humans. In his 1925 Marburg lecture course, entitled "Prolegomena to the History of the Concept of Time," he explains:

> Whether [Dasein] "is composed of" the physical, psychic, and spiritual and how these realities are to be determined is here left completely unquestioned. We place ourselves in principle outside of these experiential and interrogative horizons outlined by the definition of the most customary name for this entity: *homo animal rational*. What is to be determined is not an outward appearance of this entity but from the outset and throughout *its way to be*, not the what of that of which it is composed but the *how of its being and the characters of this how*. (HCT, 154)

Thus the inquiry into the question of being begins by describing human existence as we are everyday and for the most part, as we are already involved with workaday tools and engaged in a meaningful nexus of discursive practices, institutions, and habits. I am "thrown" (*geworfen*) into this meaningful web of relations by my concrete activity, prior to detached theorizing about the properties of objects. In this regard, the essence of Dasein is not to be found in the enduring properties or characteristics of humans. Rather, *"the essence of Dasein lies in its existence"* (BT, 67).

Existence, of course, is not to be understood in the traditional sense, in terms of static, objective "presence" (*Anwesenheit*). Existence is the dynamic temporal "movement" (*Bewegung*) or "happening" (*Geschehen*) of an understanding of being that unfolds in a concrete historical world. Dasein *is* this happening of understanding, and existence refers to the unique way that a human being understands or interprets his or her life within a shared, sociohistorical context. Thus "to *exist* is essentially . . . to *understand*" (BP, 276, emphasis added). I *am*, in the course of my everyday social activity, what I understand or interpret myself to be.[10] I have a pretheoretical or "preontological" understanding of a background of social practices.[11] I am not born with this understanding; I "grow" into it through a process of socialization, whereby I acquire the ability to interpret myself, to "take a stand" on my life (BT, 41).[12] My acts and practices, in this regard, take place within a meaningful public space or "clearing" (*Lichtung*) on the basis of which I make sense of my life and things show up for me *as* the kinds of things that they are. This context "governs" any possible interpretation that I can have of myself (HCT, 246).

Interpreting Dasein in terms of activity or movement allows us to make some preliminary remarks on the role of the body in Heidegger's project. The conception of the body as understood by mainstream Anglophone philosophy has been handed down to us from Cartesian and empiricist epistemologies, where human being is understood in terms of objective matter, of static corporeal substance (*res extensa*). In *Being and Time*, Heidegger makes it clear that one cannot think of Dasein in this way, "as a being-present-at-hand of some corporeal Thing (such as a human body) 'in' an entity that is present-at-hand" (BT, 79). This remark can be clarified by distinguishing between two senses of the body in the German language, the quantifiable "material body" (*Körper*) and the "lived-body" (*Leib*). The lived-body is not a reference to a Cartesian/Newtonian body, not a corporeal mass with measurable attributes. According to the Cartesian interpretation, bodies are defined in terms of (1) measurable weight, mass, and shape, (2) occupying a specific spatial-temporal location, and (3) having determinate boundaries.[13] Thus rocks, trees, cultural artifacts, and human beings are all instances of *Körper*, but this definition does not help us understand how humans live as embodied agents in the world. The objectifying, quantifiable approach to understanding the body is itself derived from the everyday experiences of the lived-body. In his 1936–1937 Nietzsche lectures, Heidegger articulates his rejection of the dominant naturalistic interpretation of the human body in the following way.

> We do not "have" a body in the way we carry a knife in a sheath. Neither is the body a natural body that merely accompanies us and which we can establish, expressly or not, as being also "at hand." We do not "have" a body; rather, we "are" bodily. . . . Our being embodied is essentially other than merely being encumbered with an organism. Most of what we know from the natural sciences about the body and the way it embodies are specifications based on the established misinterpretation of the body as a mere natural body. (N1, 99–100)

Heidegger fortifies this point in his 1947 "Letter on Humanism" when he writes:

> The fact that physiology and physiological chemistry can scientifically explain man as an organism is no proof that in this "organic" thing, that is, in the body scientifically explained

the essence of man consists. . . . The "essence" of man—lies
in ek-sistence [being-in-the-world]. (LH, 228–29)

The essence of Dasein, therefore, is not to be found in physiological
attributes but in existence. Thus "everything we call our bodiliness,"
says Heidegger, "down to the last muscle fiber and down to the
most hidden molecule of hormones, [already] belongs essentially to
existing" (ZS, 232). In this regard, Dasein is a term that is meant to
capture the way in which we are already concretely involved in the
world, in an average sociohistorical understanding of things, and
we can never disengage from or get clear of it. "[I] already stand in
an understanding of the 'is' [being] without being able to determine
conceptually what 'is' means. . . . This *vague average* understanding of
being is still a fact" (BT, 25). Hence, existence is not to be understood
in terms of an encapsulated body or a self-enclosed consciousness
but in terms of what Heidegger calls *"ec-stasis"* or *"ek-sistence,"* of
already "standing outside" and thereby *in* a sociohistorical world.
"Dasein has always already *stepped out beyond itself*, ex-sistere, it is
in a world. Consequently, it is never anything like a subjective inner
sphere" (BP, 170).

My *existentiell* understanding of being is not only mediated by
the fact that I have been arbitrarily thrown into a communal web of
social relations. As a temporal unfolding, my self-interpreting activity
is also finite. Because my existence is always pressing forward into
future possibilities that ultimately end with death, my understanding of being is "unfinished." As long as I exist, I am a "not yet," a
"no-thing." "[Dasein] must always, as such a potentiality, *not yet be*
something" (BT, 276). In this sense, Dasein's existence is interpreted
as a kind of nullity, because the social projects that give my life a
sense of permanence and stability are penetrated by contingency
and finitude. Heidegger is rejecting the interpretation of life as a
sequentially ordered stream of experiences that ultimately ends in
death. Life, rather, is a "movement" or "happening" that is structurally determined by the ever-present possibility of death. Death,
as a structural component of life, reveals the finitude and forward
directionality of life; it points to the possibility of my fulfillment,
even though such fulfillment is impossible.

My being, in this regard, is always unfinished or incomplete. I
can always press into other possibilities—change careers, get divorced,
or quit my job—right up until the moment of death. I only become
something when I *am no longer*, when my life is finished because I can
no longer press forward into the future. For this reason, Heidegger

identifies the primary temporal mode of life as futural. My life is structurally "on the way" (*unterwegs*), always "ahead of itself." Dasein, in this regard, is a "potentiality" that can never attain completeness or "wholeness."

> [This structural factor] tells us unambiguously that something is always *still outstanding* in Dasein, which, as a potentiality-for-being for Dasein itself, has not yet become "actual." It is essential to the basic constitution of Dasein that there is *constantly something still to be settled*. Such a lack of totality signifies that there is something still outstanding in one's potentiality-for-being. (BT, 279)

So in order to approach the question of being, I must begin with an inquiry into my own *existentiell* way of being, and this approach is determined by (1) my being arbitrarily thrown into a context of social relations that already matter to me and shape my life choices in certain ways and (2) my contingency and finitude, indicating the futural, forward-directed incompleteness of my life.

If Heidegger were merely emphasizing the priority of a finite, historically situated worldview, then this would seem to result in another form of historical or cultural relativism.[14] But this is not his aim. Heidegger's goal is to overcome relativism or "historicism" by revealing the essential structures of meaning itself, invariant a priori conditions for the possibility of any existence, any understanding of being whatsoever. For Heidegger, human existence always has a common structure:

> In this everydayness there are certain structures which we shall exhibit—not just any accidental structures, but essential ones which, in every kind of being that factical Dasein may possess, persist as determinative for its being. (BT, 38)

Thus Heidegger wants to "press on" beyond the mundane dealings of the concrete subject, to unearth "transcendental structures" that cannot be derived from any "anthropological-psychological" assumptions (KPM, 165–166). This requires what Heidegger calls "fundamental ontology," an inquiry into the "meaning of being," which "[prepares] for the question of being in general" (BT, 364). At this point, we need to address Heidegger's distinction between three types of inquiry—"ontic," "ontological," and "fundamental ontology."

Ontic investigations are concerned with particular beings (*Seiendes*). These are the investigations that can address the specific roles, attributes, or qualities of humans (being a professor, a man, a father, etc.) or the determinate properties and characteristics of nonhuman beings (being warm-blooded, carbon-based, prime, etc.). The regional sciences (mathematics, biology, theology, physics, psychology, etc.) are ontic investigations. Regional sciences often undergo ontological "crises" when there is disagreement or confusion concerning the being of the beings studied. For instance, a "crisis" takes place when theoretical physicists disagree about the being of the most elemental substances in the universe, whether or not they are particles, waves, strings, and so on. Ontological investigations can address these crises.[15]

Ontology is concerned with the being (*Sein*) of the beings studied in the regional sciences. Ontology, in this regard, addresses the essence (*essentia*) of things ("*what* something is") and the existence (*existentia*) of things ("*that* something is") (WCT, 161). According to Heidegger, the ontic sciences already operate under the tacit understanding that they grasp the ontological status of the beings that they study. Heidegger explains this problem in the following way:

> Ontic sciences in each case thematize a given entity that in a certain manner is always already disclosed prior to scientific disclosure. We call the sciences of entities as given—of a *positum*—positive sciences. . . . Ontology, or the science of being, on the other hand, demands a fundamental shift of view: From entities to being.[16]

For example, botany relies on the ontological understanding of "the vegetable character of plants," physics on "the corporeality of bodies," zoology on "the animality of animals," and so forth. Every positive science has a regional ontology, a background understanding of the being of beings it studies.[17] However, Heidegger contends that traditional ontology presupposes an understanding of being in general; it fails to ask: "What is it *to be* at all?" What is being?" According to Heidegger, this type of investigation is "*ontology taken in the broadest sense*" (BT, 31, emphasis added). Ontology in the broadest sense requires one to ask about the *meaning* of being. When we begin to question the meaning of being we are doing what Heidegger calls "fundamental ontology."

Fundamental ontology is concerned with *how* and *why* beings are intelligible or how they make sense to us in the first place. Or, more broadly conceived, it is concerned with how "meaning" (*Sinn*) itself is possible. Because humans already embody a tacit understanding of being in their everyday activities, fundamental ontology requires a phenomenological analysis of human existence, an "analytic of Dasein" or "existential analytic."[18]

> The question of the meaning of being becomes possible at all only if there is something like an understanding of being. Understanding of being belongs to the kind of being which we call "Dasein." The more appropriately and primordially we have succeeded in explicating this entity, the surer we are to attain our goal in the further course of working out the problem of fundamental ontology. (BT, 244)

"Thus *fundamental ontology*, from which alone all other ontologies can originate, must be sought in the *existential analytic of Dasein*" (BT, 34).

For Heidegger, meaning is not generated by the mental activity of a self-enclosed consciousness. Meaning emerges from the sociohistorical world that I have been thrown into and *on the basis of which* things can show up in an intelligible way. In order to grasp Heidegger's conception of meaning in terms of a context of worldly relations, it is important to understand that Dasein does not fundamentally refer to an individual. Dasein is not a self, a "pure I" (*reinen Ich*) or consciousness that is separate and distinct from surrounding objects (BT, 272). From Heidegger's perspective, human beings are not disengaged spectators but are "being-in-the-world," always already engaged in a public situation, a "*common* totality of surroundings" (HCT, 188). However, focusing on the concrete, situated activity of humans does not mean one should interpret Heidegger's conception of Dasein in terms of the framework of "existentialism" or even "existential phenomenology."[19]

Critics of Heidegger, including Edmund Husserl, Jean-Paul Sartre, Alphonse de Waelhens, Maurice Merleau-Ponty, and many contemporary commentators, often misinterpret Heidegger's use of Dasein as a reference to *a* being, that is, a subject that is concretely involved in or with its everyday social situation prior to mental reflection. These critics mistakenly label Heidegger an existentialist or a philosophical anthropologist who is primarily concerned with a descriptive analysis of situated human experience. However, this interpretation fails to appreciate Heidegger's efforts to overcome Cartesian subjectivity. For the existentialists, subjectivity was simply recast. The detached theoretical perspective that provided the Cartesian subject with an impartial "God's-eye view" of the world was replaced with an involved, situated subject whose perspective on the world was fundamentally ambiguous and contingent due to the finitude of the subject and the arbitrariness of historical conditions.

Heidegger agreed with existentialism's preliminary move away from abstract speculation, but he was continually misunderstood by existentialists for interpreting his project as a subjectivist endeavor. Sartre, in particular, is notorious for placing Heidegger within the terrain of subjectivism. Sartre insists in "Existentialism Is Humanism" (1946):

> There is at least one being whose existence comes before essence, a being which exists before it can be defined by any conception of it. That being is man or, as Heidegger has it, the human reality. . . . What [Heidegger and the French existentialists] have in common is simply the fact that they believe that existence comes before any essence—or, if you will, that we must begin from the subjective.[20]

However, Sartre's claim that philosophy must begin with the subjective, in the sense that concrete "existence" precedes all theoretical reflection about "essences," is not Heidegger's primary concern. In his "Letter on Humanism," Heidegger reminds Sartre that it is inappropriate to think of Dasein in terms of a concrete subject. Rather, "man occurs essentially in such a way that he is the 'there' [das 'Da'], that is, the lighting of being" (LH, 240). Heidegger explains his departure from Sartre and traditional translations of Dasein in the following way:

> In the philosophic tradition, the term "Dasein" means presence-at-hand, existence. In this sense, one speaks, for instance, of proofs of God's existence. However, Da-sein is understood differently in *Being and Time*. To begin with, French existentialists failed to pay attention to it. That is why they translated Da-sein in *Being and Time* as *être-la*, which means being here and not there. The *Da* in *Being and Time* does not mean a statement of place for a being, but rather it should designate the openness where beings can be present for the human being. (ZS, 120)[21]

Heidegger insists that Dasein is not to be interpreted as a concrete subject that is *être-la*, "here" in a determinate place. Dasein is "there" prior to the practical involvements of the subject. Dasein refers to a historical space or clearing of meaning on the basis of which things emerge-into-presence *as* the kinds of things they are. Conceiving of humans in terms of a space of intelligibility is crucial to understanding the aims of fundamental ontology.

In Chapter IV of Division I of *Being and Time*, Heidegger explains why Dasein should not be interpreted in terms of the concrete actions of a "subject" or "I." According to Heidegger, Dasein is more like a "mass" term that captures the way human activity is always shared, communal; "being-in-the-world" is already "being-there-with-others" (*Mit-dasein*) (BT, 152). Dasein, in this regard, is properly understood in terms of "what it does," going about its daily life, "taking a stand on itself," handling equipment, talking to friends, going to work, and getting married (BP, 159). "For the most part," as Heidegger says in *Being and Time*, "everyday Dasein understands itself in terms of that which it is customarily concerned. 'One *is*' what one does" (BT, 283). Heidegger is stressing the fact that our prereflective everyday dealings are shared. I am engaged in the acts and practices that "They" are or "Anyone" (*das Man*) is engaged in. And if I am what I do, then I *am* an indistinguishable "Anyone." When Heidegger asks "Who is it that Dasein is in everydayness?," the answer is "Anyone." "[The anyone] is the 'realist subject' of everydayness" (BT, 166). In my everyday life, I am a teacher, a husband, or a father because I have been "absorbed" (*aufgehen*) and "dispersed" (*zerstreuen*) into the discursive roles, habits, gestures, and equipment of others (BT, 167). Others assign meaning to my life. They make me who I am. Thus Dasein is "existentially" or structurally being-with-others, a "They-self" (BT, 155). But who are "They"? Heidegger explains:

> The "who" is not this one, not that one, not oneself [*man selbst*], not some people [*einige*], and not the sum of them all. The "who" is the neuter, the "They" [*das Man*]. (BT, 164)

The anonymous "They" or "Anyone" refers to a totality of interconnected relations: customs, occupations, practices, and cultural institutions as embodied in gestures, artifacts, monuments, and so forth. This totality of relations gives meaning to beings; it is on the basis of these relations that things can show up or count in determinate ways. Thus "Anyone" determines in advance the possible ways that I can understand or interpret the world (BT, 167).

Heidegger uses the analogy of activity in a "work-shop" to explain this meaningful referential context. In a workshop I do not encounter individual tools in isolation. I encounter a "totality of equipment" (*Zeugganze*) (BT, 97). My use of a hammer, for instance, is already bound to a nexus of relations, to boards, nails, a workbench, windows, lights, doors, and gloves. And I must already be familiar with the totality of equipment, as a unified context of relations, in order to encounter the hammer *as* a hammer, the nails *as* nails. This familiarity allows entities to be meaningfully disclosed *as such*.

In my everyday activities, I am already familiar with this meaningful referential context. For instance, I do not encounter my computer in isolation. The computer is significant to me only in terms of its relation to other equipment as well as to cultural institutions, future projects, and past events that have already been made available by the "Anyone." The computer sits on my desk near a lamp, and it is being used to compose an article. The article will be sent to a university and will be read by an editor of a journal. If published, this article may help me get promoted, which will secure my job and fill out my self-interpretation as a college professor. The computer means something to me only in terms of its place in a network of relations, and I have grown into this shared network by means of public norms, habits, and roles that are already there (HCT, 246). It is on the basis of this common understanding that entities are meaningful or make sense to me. Heidegger writes, "When [beings] have come to be understood—we say that they have *meaning* [*Sinn*]" (BT, 192).

> Meaning is that wherein the intelligibility [*Verständlichkeit*] of something maintains itself. Meaning is the "upon which" of a projection in terms of which something becomes intelligible as something. (BT, 193)

The public context of intelligibility always accompanies me in my various concrete engagements with entities. Thus the being of entities is always meaningful, and the context or clearing of intelligibility "nourishes" being; "it gives" (*Es gibt*) the meaning.

> If we say that entities "have meaning," this signifies that they have become accessible *in their being*. Entities "have" meaning only because they become intelligible in the projection of that being—that is to say, in terms of the "upon which" of that projection. The primary projection of the understanding of being "*gives*" the meaning. (BT, 371–72)

As a condition for the possibility of an understanding of being, meaning is a structure of Dasein (BT, 193). Human existence alone is structured by meaning, because we are thrown into a disclosive horizon that allows beings to be understood. It is for this reason that "Dasein [alone] 'has' meaning."

> Only Dasein can be meaningful [*sinnvoll*] or meaningless [*sinnlos*]. That is to say, its own being and the entities disclosed with its being can be appropriated in understanding, or can remain relegated to non-understanding. (BT, 193)

Interpreting Dasein in terms of a shared space of meaning helps explain why Heidegger rarely speaks of *a* Dasein. Dasein is a mass term that indicates a public "*Spielraum*" or "there" on the basis of which beings show up *as such*.[22] My embodied agency, in this regard, is always shaped and guided by a familiar public context. I take on roles, deal with others, and use equipment in a particular way because Dasein has opened up a meaningful network of cultural relations into which I have been absorbed.

Temporality as the Meaning of Being

Heidegger identifies a number of essential interconnected structures that constitute Dasein as a space of intelligibility. To gain access to the structures of Dasein, Heidegger begins by describing his own *existentiell* understanding of being. As a "factical" ontic being, his understanding is necessarily incomplete due to his own structural "finitude" and "thrownness." Thus the structures of understanding that Heidegger seeks are not conceptually fixed, universal "essences," ideas, or categories (FCM, 293). The structures can never be fully captured in formal concepts; we can only discover these structures by paying careful phenomenological attention to our own prereflective life experiences.[23] Thus the structures are "fundamentally undetermined"; they merely "indicate" or "point to" (*anzeigen*) general conditions that are concretely lived out by each factical Dasein (BT, 152).

These existential conditions are not "accidental" or "arbitrary"; they are "essential" because they can be concretely demonstrated in our own everyday acts and practices (BT, 37–38). For this reason, the existential analytic must start by describing one's own *existentiell* ways of being. Early on in *Being and Time*, Heidegger explains:

> The roots of the existential analysis are ultimately *existenti-ell*—that is *ontical*. Only when philosophical research is itself

seized upon in an *existentiell* manner as a possibility of the being of each existing Dasein does it become at all possible to disclose the [structural] *existentiality* of existence. (BT, 34, emphasis added)

And later, he writes:

Unless we have an *existentiell* understanding all analysis of *existentiality* will remain groundless. (BT, 360, emphasis added)

However, focusing on one's own *existentiell* understanding is problematic, precisely because our everyday ways of living "cover over" or "close off" genuine access to the structures of Dasein (BT, 359). Our individual understanding of things is always shaped in advance by the prejudices and assumptions characteristic of the social world into which we are thrown.[24]

Because human beings always already interpret themselves in terms of a background of socio-historical assumptions and prejudices, there is "circularity" to existence (BT, 363). The hermeneutic circle is not a logical problem at all. It refers to a structure of any and all self-interpreting, self-understanding activity (BT, 195). This circularity of understanding reveals that fundamental ontology has two interrelated limitations due to the "finitude" and "thrownness" of our own *existentiell* understanding. First, because our understanding is finite, fundamental ontology can never arrive at a secure, Archimedean foundation that provides an exhaustive description of what it means to be human. Second, because our understanding is thrown into a particular situation, it is constantly "corrupted" and "misleading" due to a "fore-structure," an a priori framework of historically mediated assumptions and expectations projected in advance of any individual interpretation. Hence, fundamental ontology is determined by a "hermeneutic situation" that indicates that there is no objective ground from which the essential structures of understanding become transparent (BT, 275).

Thus "[the] 'circle' belongs to the structure of meaning, and the latter phenomenon is rooted in the existential constitution of Dasein—that is, in the understanding which interprets" (BT, 195). It is the hermeneutic situation that serves as the horizon or space of meaning, allowing beings to show up or reveal themselves *as such*. And, if there is no way to theoretically disengage or get clear of the circularity of understanding, then one must "leap into this circle primordially and wholly, so that even at the start of the analysis of Dasein we make sure that we have a full view of Dasein's circular being" (BT, 363). This "leap" has a threefold purpose. First, it enables us to become aware of the contingency and arbitrariness of our hermeneutic situation. Second, it allows us to call into question the current way that things are understood or disclosed. And finally, it opens us up to the possibility of recovering a horizon of disclosure that is more "original" or "primordial" than the objectifying worldview of metaphysics (BT, 44). This "authentic" recovery is the ultimate aim of fundamental ontology.

By mapping out the structures of understanding, fundamental ontology reveals how these structures "conceal" and "obscure" an authentic understanding of being and points us in the direction of recovering an authentic understanding. This recovery can take place if we grasp the "meaning of being of Dasein" itself, which is "temporality" (*Zeitlichkeit*). Thus "time needs to be explicated primordially as the horizon for the understanding of being, and in terms of temporality as the being of Dasein, which understands being" (BT, 39). For Heidegger, beings are disclosed only in relation to time, hence, the source of our "forgetfulness" of an authentic understanding of being in the West is to be found in Dasein's own temporal constitution.

Again, fundamental ontology begins with phenomenological descriptions of the way things show themselves in the course of our everyday acts and practices. But these descriptions are merely "preparatory." The "primordial" aim of Heidegger's project is to uncover essential structures of Dasein that determine the ways in which beings show up (BT, 38). The results of this deeper, ontological inquiry will reveal that Dasein has a meaning: "temporality." Heidegger explains:

> Our analysis of Dasein is not only incomplete; it is also, in the first instance, *provisional*. It merely brings out the being of this entity, without interpreting its meaning. It is rather a preparatory procedure by which the horizon for the most primordial way of interpreting being may be laid bare. Once we have arrived at this horizon, this preparatory analytic of Dasein will have to be repeated on a higher and authentically ontological basis. . . . We shall point to *temporality* as the meaning of the being of that entity which we call "Dasein." (BT, 38)

Thus the structures of Dasein must now be "interpreted over again as modes of temporality" (BT, 38).

On the traditional view, according to Heidegger, time has been understood in Aristotelian terms as a successive sequence of "now points," which endlessly follow one after another, where one "now" is "earlier and another later" (CT, 4). This view yields "clock-time," which measures and organizes these "now points" in terms of hours, days, months, and years. And this measurement is always accomplished in reference to the "present" (CT, 17). Against this view, Heidegger argues that sequential clock-time is itself derived from and made possible by "primordial temporality." For Heidegger, this means the question "What is time?" is itself ill conceived. The more appropriate question is "Who is time?" (CT, 22).

For Heidegger, primordial temporality must be understood in terms of human existence, and existence stretches in three dimensions, from out of the "present" (*Gegenwart*), into the "future" (*Zukunft*), and back to the "past" (*Gewesenheit*). Primordial time is, therefore, understood as a holistic, nonsuccessive manifold of three dimensions or "ecstasies." In the present, I "fall prey" (*verfallen*) to the habits, roles, and assumptions of the public world as I go about my everyday life. However, my everyday involvement with things is always mediated by the "past" and the "future," by the temporal structures of "situatedness" (*Befindlichkeit*) and "projection" (*Entwurf*). Situatedness refers to the way in which I am arbitrarily thrown into a shared world, with a shared history that attunes or affects me in terms of particular dispositions or "moods" (*Stimmung*). Projection refers to the way I prereflectively understand my workaday activities as I press forward into future goals and projects, into the "for-the-sake-of-which" (*das Worumwillen*). It is only on the basis of this disclosive horizon—one that, out of the present, simultaneously reaches *forward* into social possibilities and projects that are "not yet" and *backward* into a shared situation that allows things to count and matter in particular ways—that beings can emerge-into-presence *as such*.

Although we will return to this question in later chapters, we can see how the body might initially be implicated in the structure of *Befindlichkeit*, because the experience of our socio-historical situation is disclosed to us in terms of embodied moods.[25] If this is true, then it appears that the body should be interpreted as an essential structure of meaning.[26] However, this suggestion puts too much emphasis on the role of the individual subject in terms of mood formation, and it fails to distinguish between my own embodied agency and the disclosive horizon that is already "there," a horizon that already gives meaning to my activities.

Heidegger's use of *Stimmung* is not to be understood subjectively where the world meaningfully affects me in terms of my own psychological "states of mind," being depressed, afraid, bored, or excited. Rather, *Stimmung* is the condition for the possibility of any individual disposition or mood. The mood is not in *me,* in the body; I am already in a mood by virtue of my public involvements, by being thrown into a shared social context that determines in advance the way things affect me. In short, mood is "like an atmosphere," already "there" prior to the emergence of the body, and it is by means of this atmosphere that my embodied engagements are tuned or disposed in one way or another toward things. In his 1929–1930 lectures, Heidegger says:

> Moods are *not side-effects,* but are something which in advance determines our being with one another. It seems as though moods [are] in each case already there, so to speak, like an *atmosphere* in which we first immerse ourselves in each case and which then attunes us through and through. (FCM, 67)

Hence, moods are both a priori and public, making it possible for me, as an embodied agent, to be in a mood.

> The dominance of the public way in which things have been interpreted has already been decisive even for the possibilities of having a [mood]—that is, for the basic way in which Dasein lets the world "matter" to it. (BT, 213)

For Heidegger, moods reveal the way communal events, roles, occupations, and equipment already matter to us. For instance, the practices of a teacher, husband, or father matter to me because they are part of the world with which I am familiar, whereas the practices of a shaman, witch doctor, or tribal chief do not show up in terms of this familiar nexus of social relations, and therefore they do not shape the future course of my life. Thus moods disclose a basic temporal structure of Dasein, the structure of "alreadiness," that is prior to my own embodied agency. Heidegger puts it in the following way:

> Why can I let a pure thing of the world be encountered at all in bodily presence? Only because the world is *already there* in thus letting it be encountered. . . . I can see a natural thing in its bodily presence only on the basis of this being-in-the-world. (HCT, 196, emphasis added)

It is only if our embodied acts and practices are structured by the past, by situatedness, that we can be tuned to the world in the first place. We can say that the body gives us access to intraworldly things and is, therefore, required for any human being to be in a mood, but the body does not constitute the meaningfulness of moods or make them possible. Moods, like the world itself, are already there for us to grow into.

To this end, Heidegger's phenomenological description of our embodied understanding of things is only the first step in his program. His core concern is the original horizon of meaning itself. In this more primordial sense, Dasein is to be understood as the *Da-sein*, as the "being of the-there," the clearing that makes possible meaningful bodily acts and practices. Here the emphasis is not on the particular embodied engagements of the individual but on temporality as the "*Da*," the disclosive space or "openness" that lets beings show up in their being. It is for this reason that Heidegger, in his 1928 Leibniz lectures, refers to Dasein's openness as "neutral," because it is prior to the body, "prior to every factual concretion" (MFL, 136). It is what makes possible "bodiliness," "sexuality," and "concrete factual human-ity." As embodied agents, we already "stretch along" forward and backward in a disclosive temporal horizon (MFL, 137–38).

As we will see in the proceeding chapters, the critical questions concerning Dasein's embodied agency, our perceptual capacities, our sexed and gendered specificity, and our animal nature are important only to the extent that they give us access to the question of the meaning of being. But this kind of questioning—and any mode of comportment, for that matter— is itself already guided in advance by temporality. "Temporality," says Heidegger, "makes possible Dasein's comportment as comportment toward beings, whether toward itself, toward others, or toward the handy or the extent" (BP, 318). In the fol-lowing, we will see that the lived-body *ek-sists* by "standing outside" of itself insofar as it is concretely engaged with a public world. As such, the embodied agent transcends the traditional binary of subject and object, surpassing the boundaries of his or her own skin as he or she shapes and is shaped by intraworldly beings. But this transcendence is made meaningful by temporality. Time, in this regard, is to be seen as the origin of any meaningful possibility whatsoever, and, as such, it is "earlier" than any bodily comportment (BP, 325).

The Missing Dialogue between Heidegger and Merleau-Ponty

In September 1959, Heidegger began a series of lectures with physicians and psychiatrists at the University of Zurich's medical clinic, Burghölzli. The austere, technological appearance of the new auditorium was not to Heidegger's liking, and the seminars moved to the house of one of Heidegger's close friends and colleagues, Medard Boss, who lived in Zollikon. These seminars continued for more than a decade, and it is during this period that Heidegger, for the first time, engaged French critics who had attacked his failure to offer a thematic account of the body in *Being and Time*. Unfortunately, Heidegger's critical response is primarily directed toward Jean-Paul Sartre and makes no reference to Merleau-Ponty. This is frustrating, given the fact that Heidegger's account of the body in the Zollikon seminars is strikingly similar to Merleau-Ponty's.[1]

It is unfortunate that no productive exchange takes place between the two, because Merleau-Ponty reveals a crucial misstep in Heidegger's early work by addressing the fundamental role that the body plays in spatially orienting our worldly acts and practices. In *Being and Time*, there is no acknowledgment of the body that prereflectively negotiates its way through the world, a body that is already oriented in terms of directionality as it reaches out and faces the various tools and others that are encountered every day. The goal of this chapter is to draw on the parallels of the Zollikon seminars and Merleau-Ponty's phenomenology in order to see how Heidegger's neglect of the body affects his early project of fundamental ontology and to determine whether or not an account of the body is necessary to complete the project.

The Absence of the Body in *Being and Time*

Again, Heidegger's reluctance to offer an account of the body in *Being and Time* should not be surprising if we understand his motivation for undermining the assumption of substance ontology that dominates the Western philosophic tradition. This ontology interprets all things—trees, animals, sounds, numbers, ideas, humans—in terms of substance, where substance refers to that which endures or remains the same through any change in properties. This view took its definitive modern form with Descartes's bifurcation between mind/thinking substance (*res cogitans*) and body/extended substance (*res extensa*). Today, the importance of an immaterial mind has diminished, and mainstream philosophers have, for the most part, adopted the standpoint of "materialism," that everything that exists is physical substance of one kind or another.

In chapter 1 we saw that the picture of the body that we inherit from the Cartesian tradition can only be understood in terms of its opposition to an immaterial mind; it is a material substance that has several essential qualities. It occupies a particular location in a spatial container, thus the body has determinate boundaries and can be at only one place at a time, "here and not there" (ZS, 120). It has observable, quantifiable measurements. And it is regarded as an object in the Latin sense of *ob-jectum*, something that is set before and represented by the theorizing subject. Undoing the assumptions of modern materialism is one of the goals of *Being and Time*. Here Heidegger is not concerned with focusing on the properties of objects that are theoretically examined by the detached subject. Rather, he wants to turn our attention to the ordinary activity of human existence itself that underlies and makes possible any and all theorizing.

According to Heidegger, we are already thrown into a shared sociohistorical world, and in the course of our workaday lives, there is no inner/outer relation, no subjective mental intention that affects an independent, material world of objects. For instance, I am not thematically aware of the "handy" (*zuhanden*) things that I use as I go through my day: I open doors, drive cars, and type on computers without a reflective act of consciousness. Any detached, theoretical awareness of the objective properties of things is derivative, already taking place against a background of practical awareness, of prereflective *know-how*. Heidegger's analysis of everyday activity reveals that in the flow of my working life, I am not a subject theoretically set over and against objects; rather, as "being-in-the-world," I am *ec-static*: I "stand outside" of myself because I am always already woven into things in terms of a tacit, practical familiarity. Thus I am "in" the world not in terms of occupying a spatial location in a three-dimensional coordinate system; rather, "*being-in*" (*in-sein*) is to be interpreted in the existential sense of involvement, such as "being in love," "being in school," or "being in the army."

On this point, Heidegger and Merleau-Ponty are in agreement. The human being is not a substance at all but is rather the dynamic activity or "movement" (*Bewegung*) of life. In this regard, the objectified picture of the self that appears in theoretical reflection is derivative from the way of being that characterizes our prereflective, practical dealings with the environing world. In this respect, although Merleau-Ponty claims phenomenological allegiance to Husserl, he clearly has a great deal in common with Heidegger. On the one hand, Heidegger and Merleau-Ponty agree with Husserl that (1) phenomenology studies or describes the domain of prescientific, pre-objective human experience, and (2) intentional directedness is essential to the experience of human existence. On the other hand, Heidegger and Merleau-Ponty reject Husserl's dualistic view that experience involves an *immanent* mental content distinct from our encounter with a *transcendent*, outer reality. According to Heidegger and Merleau-Ponty, our experience of the world cannot be understood in terms of intentional acts in which meanings are bestowed on "objects-as-experienced." Rather, in their view, human beings are always already concretely involved in the world. Thus intentionality should refer to the situated activity or "comportment" (*Verhalten*) that necessarily precedes the theoretical operations of consciousness. Heidegger explains:

> The usual [Husserlian] conception of intentionality misunderstands . . . the structure of the self-directedness toward, the intention. This misinterpretation lies in an erroneous subjectivising of intentionality. . . . The idea of a subject which has intentional experiences merely inside its own sphere and is not yet outside it but encapsulated within itself is an absurdity which misconstrues the basic ontological structure of the being that we ourselves are. (BP, 63–64)

Whereas, for Husserl, the structures of intentionality are located within the subjective inner sphere of consciousness, Heidegger and Merleau-Ponty contend that such a sphere is too Cartesian and is derivative from everyday, prethematic involvements that are prior to inner/outer distinctions. Merleau-Ponty confirms this point when he writes:

> Truth does not "inhabit" only the "inner man" or more accurately, there is no inner man; man is in the world, and

> only in the world does he know himself. When I return to
> myself from an excursion into the realm of dogmatic com-
> mon sense or of science, I find, not a source of intrinsic
> truth, but a subject destined to the world. (PP, xi)

We are already engaged in a concrete situation in such a way that it
is impossible to sever this preobjectifying bond between human and
world in order to "remake" it in terms of the constituting powers of
the transcendental ego. For Heidegger and Merleau-Ponty, phenomenology uncovers this primordial interconnection, awakening us to
our prior situatedness, our inherence in the world. Merleau-Ponty
says, "Looking for the world's essence is not looking for what is an
idea once it has been reduced to a theme of discourse; it is looking
for what it is as a fact for us, before thematisation" (PP, xiv).

For both thinkers, interpreting human being in terms of practical activity rather than in terms of substance undermines the domi-
nance of contemporary materialism. Based on their view, my being
cannot be understood in terms of measurable mass that occupies a
particular location. Rather, I understand myself primarily in terms
of my concrete concerns, my everyday doing and acting. In these
activities, my being does not have determinate boundaries; it does
not end with my own skin. As I work in my office, for instance, my
body is woven to a particular spatial region of concern—the glasses
on my face, the computer on the desk, the coffee cup, the landscape
that appears through my office window, and so forth. In this regard,
my own individual acts and practices are merely "crossing points"
or "place holders" in an interconnected network of social relations.[2]
Pierre Bourdieu explains this point from the perspective of cultural anthropology, arguing that individual acts and practices are
simply "structural variants" of a background network of relations,
a public "*habitus*."

> Since the history of the individual is never anything other
> than a certain specification of the collective history of his
> group or class, each individual system of dispositions may
> be seen as a structural variant of all the other group or
> class *habitus*.[3]

My activities are an embodiment of the "Anyone," because I have
grown into and become familiar with a public context. Thus in my
everyday doing and acting, I take on roles, deal with others, and use
equipment in a meaningful way, because the "Anyone" has opened

up a meaningful network of cultural relations, a space of intelligibility into which I have been absorbed.

Critics argue that what is missing from Heidegger's account of everyday doing and acting is an inquiry into the phenomenon of embodiment itself, an analysis of the moving body that is already spatially oriented and involved in/with things, that handles the various tools and performs the mundane tasks of everydayness. Heidegger appears to take for granted the fact that the human body is already "alive," handling, sensing, and perceiving intraworldly things in a particular way. Again, the lived-body is not a corporeal substance extended in space, and it cannot be scientifically observed from a distance, because it is already spatially involved, maneuvering through rooms, handling equipment, sensing who or what is in front or behind, and so forth. The body is already "in the way" as the original source of all practical comportment. Because of his failure to discuss the role of the lived-body in our everyday acts and practices, critics such as Hubert Dreyfus have asserted that Heidegger's account of worldly involvement is "unsatisfying," and Tina Chanter refers to it as "disembodied."[4] Alphonse de Waelhens explains the problem in the following way:

> Heidegger always situates himself at a level of complexity which permits imagining that the problem which concerns us here is resolved. For it is at the level of perception and the sensible that this problem must receive its decisive treatment. But the projects which, according to *Being and Time*, engender the intelligibility of the real for us already presuppose that the subject of daily existence raises his arm, since he hammers and builds; that he orients himself, since he drives an automobile. That a human existent can accomplish these different tasks raises no difficulty once his capacity to act and move his body, once his faculty of perceiving, have been judged "evident."[5]

At this point, we can turn to the phenomenology of Merleau-Ponty in order to see how the lived-body is already assumed in Heidegger's account of spatiality.

The Body and the Problem of Spatiality

In section 23 of *Being and Time*, Heidegger reminds us that it is a mistake to interpret the "being-in" of humans in terms of *a* being located in a particular place. My location is not to be regarded as a static spatial position that I currently occupy. Rather, it is to be understood in terms of my own *existentiell* involvement with things "at hand," things that I "bring near" in my daily activities.

> Dasein is "in" in the world in the sense that it deals with entities encountered within-the-world, and does so concernfully and with familiarity. So if spatiality belongs to it in any way, that is possible only because of this being-in. (BT, 138)

In my everyday activities, I bring things into a handy equipmental nexus, things that are "near" as I "reach for" the door, "grab" the telephone, or "look at" the clock on the wall (BT, 140–41). Thus equipment does not occupy an objective place at a measurable distance from other equipment; distance is understood in the context of familiar accessibility, where equipment is "near" or "far" in terms of being "to hand" (*zur Hand*), available for use (BT, 135). During my everyday practices, I am already familiar with where things are; the phone is not five feet away, it is "over there," and the remote control is "close by."

> Every entity that is "to hand" has a different nearness, which is not to be ascertained by measuring distances. This nearness regulates itself in terms of circumspectively "calculative" manipulating and using. (BT, 135)

Consequently, I am located in a regional nexus by being actively involved with accessible things. I am "here" or "there" only because I am currently engaged in a public, equipmental space (BT, 142). And my accessibility to things is constantly changing as I go about my daily tasks. Yet the fact that I dwell in a familiar lived-space and am involved with handy things that are "nearby" and "far away" remains constant. I am always engaged in a spatial horizon, and this horizon is itself constituted by my concrete involvements. Without such involvements, things could not be encountered spatially; thus in my everyday acts and practices, I am always already spatial.

> Space is not to be found in the subject, nor does the subject observe the world "as if" that world were in a space; but the "subject" (Dasein) if well understood ontologically, is spatial. (BT, 146)

As spatial, I encounter things in terms of an orientation, in terms of directions of right/left, front/back, up/down, and so forth. It is "out of this orientation," Heidegger says, "[that] arise the fixed directions of right and left. Dasein constantly takes these directions along with it" (BT, 143). In my everyday dealings, I am already oriented in the world, because I have grown into an understanding of a shared region of involvement. I already know my way around. However, Heidegger's analysis does not account for the body's role in this spatial orientation. One may want to ask Heidegger: Is it not the body that has been habitually interwoven to a familiar region, automatically knowing what is to the left or to the right? Is it not this reflexive body that walks me to the kitchen in the middle of the night when I need a drink of water? Does it not already know where the door is, where the refrigerator is, where the light switch is, and so on? According to Merleau-Ponty, our everyday doing and acting is made possible by the prereflective know-how of the "habit body" (*corps habituel*).

For Merleau-Ponty, our worldly involvements require a "prepersonal" body or "habit-body" that is already habitually "geared" to intraworldly things in a specific way (PP, 84). The body's engagements are "prepersonal" or prerational because they require neither inner mental intentions that constitute the world (as the rationalist tradition contends) nor a subjective consciousness receiving sense impressions from external objects (as the empiricist tradition contends). The body already has a "tacit knowledge" of its place in the world, because it has been habitually interwoven into a familiar, concrete situation. The habit body is bound to a "phenomenal field" prior to thematic inner/outer distinctions. This field is the familiar setting where intraworldly things and embodied perceptions "intersect." Merleau-Ponty writes:

> The phenomenological world is not pure being, but the sense which is revealed where the paths of my various experiences intersect, and also where my own and other people's intersect and engage each other like gears. (PP, xx)

And the body's tacit knowledge is always prior to an objective awareness of things.

> Our bodily experience of movement . . . provides us with a way of access to the world and the object, with a "*praktognosia*" [practical knowledge], which has to be recognized as original and perhaps primary. My body has its world,

or understands its world without having to make any "symbolic" or "objectifying" function. (PP, 140–41)

According to Merleau-Ponty, in my everyday practices, my lived-body is an active, dynamic synthesis of prereflective intentions as I move through a room or hail a cab from a crowded sidewalk. The body, in this regard, has a kinesthetic understanding for seamlessly maneuvering through a world, already knowing what is to the left and to the right, what is behind and in front. This is because the perceptions of the body are already situated, already oriented, and this orientation is inseparable from everyday involvement. For Merleau-Ponty, the body's prethematic orienting capacity—which forms an interconnected system with the surrounding world—is an essential and a necessary condition for worldly activity.

> Our own body is in the world as the heart is in the organism: it keeps the visible spectacle alive; it breathes life into it and sustains it inwardly, and with it forms a system. (PP, 115)

Human existence, therefore, requires a body that already understands its way around a world. Hence, "The possession of the body [already] implies the ability to 'understand' space" (PP, 251).

Heidegger's analysis completely overlooks the fundamental role that the body plays in our everyday practices. He fails to see that our ability to know our way around a situation depends on a body, revealing why we must "face" things in order to meaningfully deal with them in the first place.[6] To maneuver through a world depends upon the body's *praktognosia* of spatial directionality and orientation, of where it is within a nexus of relations.

The Importance of the Zollikon Seminars

In the Zollikon seminars, which begin thirty-three years after the publication of *Being and Time*, Heidegger responds to this problem by turning his attention to French critics, primarily Jean-Paul Sartre, who "wondered why [Heidegger] only wrote six lines on the body in the whole of *Being and Time*" (ZS, 231). Sartre was particularly suspicious of Heidegger's neglect of the body's role in everyday social practices, leaving him "wholly unconvinced."[7] Heidegger responds by arguing that Sartre's conception of the body is still caught within the Cartesian/Newtonian tradition, regarding the body as an objective material thing with measurable properties. Heidegger contends that this is due to the fact that "the French have no word whatsoever for the body, but only a term for a corporeal thing, namely, *le corps*" (ZS, 89). For Heidegger, corporeality merely indicates that the body is physically present (*körperhaft*). It fails to see the phenomenological problem of the body, namely, that we are "there" in a "bodily" (*leibhaft*) manner.

For Heidegger, interpreting the body in terms of *Körper* rather than *Leib* overlooks the everyday way that humans are already embodied, already spatially involved with things. In speaking to medical doctors at the University of Zurich, Heidegger explains that this bodily way of being is obscured by the objective accounts of the body offered by the natural sciences, and that our everyday "layman" descriptions are actually closer to capturing the phenomenon:

> When you have back pains, are they of a spatial nature? What kind of spatiality is peculiar to the pain spreading across your back? Can it be equated with the surface extension of a material thing? The diffusion of pain certainly exhibits the character of extension, but this does not involve a surface. Of course, one can also examine the body as a corporeal thing [*Körper*]. Because you are educated in anatomy and physiology as doctors, that is, with a focus on the examination of bodies, you probably look at the states of the body in a different way than the "layman" does. Yet, a layman's experience is probably closer to the phenomenon of pain as it involves our body lines, even if it can hardly be described with the aid of our usual intuition of space. (ZS, 84)

Heidegger wants to make it clear that the body, understood phenomenologically, is not a bounded corporeal thing that is "present-at-hand" (*vorhanden*); rather, it is already stretching beyond its own skin, actively directed toward and interwoven with the world. Heidegger refers to the intentionality of our bodily nature as the " 'bodying forth' (*leiben*) of the body" (ZS, 86). And it is here that Heidegger makes contact with Merleau-Ponty.

For both thinkers, space is not to be understood in the traditional sense, as a container within which objects of experience reside. This view continues to regard the body as a corporeal thing that is disengaged from the world. For Heidegger and Merleau-Ponty, the body, as it is lived, is already engaged in a particular situation. Consequently, the boundaries of *Leib* "extend beyond" *Körper*. Heidegger explains:

> The difference between the limits of the corporeal thing
> and the body consists in the fact that the *bodily limit* is
> extended beyond the *corporeal limit*. Thus the difference
> between the limits is a quantitative one. But if we look at
> the matter in this way, we will misunderstand the very
> phenomenon of the body and of bodily limit. The bodily
> limit and the corporeal limit are not quantitative but rather
> qualitatively different from each other. The corporeal thing,
> as corporeal, cannot have a limit which is similar to the
> body at all. (ZS, 86)

For Heidegger and Merleau-Ponty, the spatial world is not a "receptacle";
rather, the body constitutes spatiality in its everyday movements.

> I walk by occupying space. The table does not occupy space
> in the same way. The human being makes space for him-
> self. He allows space to be. An example: When I move, the
> horizon recedes. The human being moves within a horizon.
> This does not only mean to transport one's body. (ZS, 16)

I "allow space to be" because I am already involved in/with
a shared, familiar environment, already engaged with the things
"around" me.

> Even if we deny that Dasein has any "insideness" [*Inwendig-
> keit*] in a spatial receptacle, this does not in principle exclude
> it from having any spatiality at all, but merely keeps open
> the way for seeing the kind of spatiality which is constitu-
> tive of Dasein. . . . We must show how the "aroundness"
> of the environment . . . *is not* present-at-hand in space. (BT,
> 134, emphasis added)

I encounter things spatially because my body is already perceptually
bound to the world; I already embody a particular way of being-in-
the-world. Heidegger writes:

> To encounter the ready-to-hand in its environmental space
> remains ontically possible only because Dasein itself is "spa-
> tial" with regard to its being-in-the-world . . . Dasein . . . is
> "in" the world in the sense that it deals with beings
> encountered within-the-world, and does so concernfully
> and with [prereflective] familiarity. So if spatiality belongs

to it in any way, that is possible only because of this being-in. (BT, 138)

Merleau-Ponty makes a similar point by touting the primacy of perception.

> [One] can convey the idea of space only if already involved in it, and if it is already known. Since perception is initiation into the world, and since, as has been said with insight, "there is nothing anterior to it which is mind," we cannot put into it objective relationships which are not yet constituted at its level. (PP, 257)

Based on this view, the body is *not* a material thing that occupies a current position in space; rather, it indicates a "range" or horizon within which a nexus of things is encountered.

> The "here" of [Dasein's] current factical situation never signifies a position in space, but signifies rather the leeway [*Spielraum*] of the range of that equipmental whole with which it is most closely concerned. (BT, 420)

Bodily perception stretches beyond the corporeal by constituting the horizon within which human beings are already oriented.

> The corporeal limit . . . cannot ever become a bodily limit itself. When pointing with my finger toward the crossbar of the window over there, I [as body] do not end at my fingertips. Where then is the limit of the body? "Each body is my body." As such, the proposition is nonsensical. (ZS, 86)

This "bodily limit," the horizon constituted by perception, is constantly changing as we "body-forth," as we maneuver through familiar situations in our everyday dealings, while the "corporeal limit" remains the same.

> The limit of bodying forth (the body is only as it is bodying forth: "body") is the horizon of being within which I sojourn [*aufhalten*]. Therefore, the limit of bodying forth changes constantly through the change in the reach of my sojourn. In contrast [then], the limit of the corporal thing usually does not change. (ZS, 87)

The constant changing of our practical horizon occurs while the body maintains its perceptual grip on the world, because the body is always situated. For Merleau-Ponty, this explains how we are able to constantly keep our balance as we walk into new settings; the perceptual body is fastened to the world and continues to encounter intraworldly things in terms of front/back, right/left, and up/down. Things are encountered prereflectively by "bodying-forth" not in terms of objective distance (i.e., the table is ten feet away) or geometrical measurements (i.e., the door is five feet wide); rather, they are initially encountered in terms of regional familiarity. Distance is not an external relationship between things but already understood in terms of preobjective involvement, in terms of the constant dialectical interplay between the "bodying-forth" of the body and the things that it encounters. The standpoint of the natural sciences presupposes this tacit understanding of measurement and distance. Heidegger explains:

> The natural scientist as such is not only unable to make a distinction between the psychical and the somatic regarding their measurability or unmeasurability. He can make no distinctions of this kind *whatsoever*. He can only distinguish among objects, the measurements of which are different in degree [quantity]. For he can only measure, and thereby he always already presupposes measurability. (ZS, 199)

Although this tacit understanding is measurably "imprecise" and "variable," it is wholly intelligible within an already familiar social context (BT, 140). In order to explain the objective properties, size, or dimensions of things, there must be a momentary breakdown or disturbance in the bodily grip that makes the skillful flow of everyday activity possible. The immediate and direct contact that the body has with the world must come to an end in order for the objective size, properties, and dimensions of things to appear. For example, in the flow of my everyday life, I use a key to open my car door. It is only when I mistakenly use the wrong key that this flow breaks down and I actually become aware of my hands, the size of my keys, and the location of the door handle. I quickly look at my hands, deliberately sift through my key chain, insert the proper key, and drive away. In this momentary breakdown, I am forced to consciously decontextualize or isolate things from their relational nexus of involvement, and it is only in doing so that the objective qualities of things emerge. To this end, any act of conscious deliberation is always derivative from the practical, prethematic bond between body and world.

Here, a related point of contact between Merleau-Ponty and Heidegger is revealed in the way the two interpret bodily movements, gestures, and expressions as already understood in terms of a meaningful social nexus. Our embodied social habits immediately inform us of what is going on in particular situations before we can begin to consciously reflect upon them. For example, the confused expression on one's face in a philosophy class does not directly reveal the objective presence of a nervous system's impulse; rather,what is revealed is an embodied look of consternation, which indicates that a difficult philosophical topic is being explored by the professor. Heidegger says:

> I just saw Dr. K. was "passing" his hand over his forehead. And yet I did not observe a change of location and position of one of his hands, but I immediately noticed that he was thinking of something difficult. (ZS, 88)

The context of social familiarity within which embodied engagements are experienced allows for a meaning or an intelligibility to emerge that is prior to mental deliberations.

We now see that Heidegger's Zollikon seminars succeed in filling out the account of embodied agency implied in *Being and Time* and reveal a kinship with Merleau-Ponty on several key points. First, the self is not regarded, fundamentally, as an enclosed consciousness that constitutes and sustains the world by inner, mental activity. Rather, in the course of our everyday doing and acting, we are already "standing outside" of ourselves by being practically engaged in a concrete situation. Second, intraworldly beings are not understood as objectified material substance with measurable locations but as entities that the embodied agent is already amidst in terms of practical orientation and familiarity. And, third, our bodily being should not be interpreted in terms of bounded material (*Körper*). In our everyday dealings, our bodily being stretches beyond the skin to the things with which we are currently concerned.

What Heidegger and Merleau-Ponty offer is a phenomenological description of embodied agency that applies to human acts and practices *generally*, as we live them *"proximally and for the most part*—in average everydayness" (BT, 37–38). However, what is not addressed in their analyses is the way in which *particular* social practices guide and shape the experience of lived-space. Iris Marion Young and Pierre Bourdieu, for instance, reveal how spatiality and motility are experienced differently along gender lines—that there are "masculine" and "feminine" comportments and orientations. Young writes:

> The young girl acquires many subtle habits of feminine body comportment—walking like a girl, tilting her head like a girl, standing and sitting like a girl, gesturing like a girl, and so on. The girl learns to hamper her movements. She is told that she must be careful not to get hurt, not to get dirty, not to tear her clothes. . . . The more a girl assumes her status as feminine, the more she takes herself to be fragile and immobile and the more she actively enacts her own body inhibition.[8]

Although we will explore this issue in more detail in chapter 3, we can follow Young's lead by suggesting that this gendered difference is evident in the way the "man" walks decisively, makes steady eye contact, has a firm handshake, speaks loudly, and dominates a circle of conversation, while the "woman" lowers her head, has a soft handshake, does not talk but smiles, listens, and nods attentively. Thus it can be argued that lateral space shrinks or expands in terms of a tacit domination in the social order.[9] As children, we grow into and master the social practices—unique to class, gender, ethnicity, disability, sexuality—and these practices, in turn, guide the ways in which we comport ourselves and move through the world. Bourdieu suggests that we can simply observe the actions of men and women dining at a fine restaurant for an example of this social order. "A man should [eat] with his whole mouth [and body] wholeheartedly, and not, like women, just with the lips, that is halfheartedly, with reservation and restraint."[10] The act of public dining reveals the way that "man" embodies an orientation in space that is expansive and uninhibited, while "woman" embodies spatial inhibition, holding her arms close to herself, sitting a certain way, crossing her legs, and quietly chewing her food.

Merleau-Ponty and Heidegger suggest that the lived-body should be conceived not as an object with measurable properties but rather as the original spatial "openness" onto the world that underlies subject/object distinctions. The body, says Merleau-Ponty, is "pure presence to the world and openness to its possibilities" (PP, 148). However, bodily movements, gestures, and expressions also indicate a social position and identity that may not represent pure openness but a form of "immanence" that is trapped within objective space. Indeed, there are inhibiting social practices that close off and restrict access to lived-space, where one comes to interpret oneself as *Körper*, as a mere body or thing, an object of another's intentions. Young makes the following case:

> An essential part of the situation of being a woman is that of living the ever-present possibility that one will be gazed upon as a mere body, as shape and flesh that presents itself as the potential object of another subject's intentions and manipulations, rather than as a living manifestation of action and intention. The source of this objectified bodily existence is in the attitude of others regarding her, but the woman herself often actively takes up her body as a mere thing. She gazes at it in the mirror, worries about how it looks to others, prunes it, shapes it, molds it, decorates it.[11]

Introducing variations of difference to the discussion of spatiality can deepen the original insights of Heidegger and Merleau-Ponty. Certainly the body is to be understood, at the deepest level, in terms of *Leib*, as concretely engaged in the norms, customs, and habits of a surrounding world, but the world that we grow into can also confine and restrict the way lived-space is experienced. Thus, it can be argued that investigations into how the body and spatiality meaningfully show up in terms of specific cultural and historical practices are crucial to the social theory and phenomenology of the body. However, I want to suggest that such investigations have little to do with Heidegger's core concern, which is fundamental ontology. At this point, we can begin to discuss the motivations and goals that separate Merleau-Ponty's project from Heidegger's, and this will, in turn, enable us to see the contribution of the Zollikon seminars in their proper light.

The Limits of Merleau-Ponty's Relation to Heidegger

For Heidegger, the Zollikon seminars serve a particular purpose, namely, to engage the medical sciences, primarily psychiatry and psychology, from the perspective of Dasein. Heidegger argues that these disciplines have adopted a traditional, Cartesian interpretation of the self and uncritically assume the event of "being-in-the-world." "As for the French [psychologists]," says Heidegger, "I am always disturbed by [their] misinterpretation of being-in-the-world; it is conceived either as being present-at-hand or as the intentionality of subjective consciousness" (ZS, 272). Heidegger's analysis of the body in these seminars is an attempt to undo the prevailing naturalistic account of the body as objective, material presence in order to come to grips with bodily being as it is lived.

> The human being's bodily being can never, fundamentally never, be considered merely as something present-at-hand if one wants to consider it in an appropriate way. If I postulate human bodily being as something present-at-hand, I have already beforehand destroyed the body *as* body. (ZS, 170, emphasis added)

The question, for our purposes, is whether this analysis of the body is needed to complete Heidegger's project of fundamental ontology, that is, whether such a project is insufficient or incomplete without such an account. I want to suggest that the analysis of the body in the Zollikon seminars is an example of regional ontology, one that identifies and describes the essential attributes of *a* particular being, in this case the lived-body. Merleau-Ponty's *Phenomenology of Perception* is a similar kind of inquiry. But the primary goal of Heidegger's early project is fundamental ontology, a form of inquiry that seeks to identify the essential—*ontological-existential*—structures that make it possible for us to make sense of any and all beings, including ourselves. These structures constitute the *Da*, the disclosive site in which any entity whatsoever can show up *as such*. This is why Heidegger claims that it is a mistake to interpret Da-sein as "*être-là*," as a being that is "here" in a determinate place. Keeping in mind this distinction between regional ontology and fundamental ontology, we can identify four overlapping points that separate Heidegger's project from Merleau-Ponty's.

First, Merleau-Ponty is primarily focused on recovering the pre-reflective bond between body and world that has been passed over by the bifurcated subject/object models that modern philosophy has inherited from rationalism and empiricism. According to Merleau-Ponty, the body is inseparable from the world, because the world is simply what my body perceives, and the objects that I perceive are always perceived in reference to my body. Embodied perception orients me in the world, making it possible for me to move toward things, to open doors, handle tools, shake the hand of a colleague, and so forth. It is on the basis of this tacit, bodily intentionality that a unified horizon is opened up between incarnate subject and worldly object. Thus Merleau-Ponty's conception of "*être-au-monde*" is perhaps best translated as "being-*towards*-the-world" rather than "being-*in*-the-world." The body-subject is always pointing beyond itself because it is already perceptually bound to worldly objects.

Heidegger's conception of Dasein as "being-in-the-world" (*In-der-Welt-sein*) is a radical departure from *être-au-monde*. For Heidegger, Dasein is not a subject that is perceptually bound to worldly objects. Dasein *is* the world, the "Anyone," the relational nexus of customs, habits, norms, and institutions *on the basis of which* things show up *as such* in embodied comportment. Dasein, as a meaningful public context, is already there, prior to bodily perception. It is the condition for the possibility of any meaningful perception whatsoever. Because I *ek-sist* within this disclosive context, I do not perceive things in isolation. I perceive them in terms of a holistic clearing with which I am already familiar. I interpret myself as a student, a teacher, or a husband because I am familiar with certain public practices, gestures, and equipment that enable me to make sense of my life. My individual activities are simply crossing points in the coherent social patterns and relations of the "Anyone," and the "Anyone" makes possible meaningful activities and perceptions.

Second, it can be argued that what is presupposed by Merleau-Ponty is an inquiry into the conditions for the possibility of meaning itself, which would explain *how* and *why* the perceptions of the body-subject make sense or are intelligible. Merleau-Ponty introduces terms such as "field," "background," "horizon," "fabric," and "world" that hint at Heidegger's conception of Dasein as a disclosive space of meaning. For instance, Merleau-Ponty writes:

> Perception is not a science of the world, it is not even an act, a deliberate taking up of a position; it is the background from which all acts stand out, and is presupposed by them. The world is not an object such that I have in my possession the law of its making; it is the natural setting of, and field for, all my thoughts and all my explicit perception. . . . [The] *Sinngebung*, or active meaning-giving operation which may be said to define consciousness, so . . . *the world is nothing but "world-as-meaning."* (PP, xi)

Yet Merleau-Ponty never explains "world-as-meaning." Is Merleau-Ponty referring to a cultural world, historical world, natural world, physical world, and so on? Is the "cultural world" also a "natural setting?" And, if so, how does this world *give* meaning? These questions remain unanswered in Merleau-Ponty and, because he holds onto a conception of subjectivity, one is left to wonder if meaning is, as it is for Husserl, ultimately discovered and constituted "in me," in "incarnate consciousness" (PP, xiii). For Heidegger, the source of meaning is already grounded in the shared background that human beings grow into. Heidegger's account of the background of intelligibility as the origin or source of meaning is what Merleau-Ponty's phenomenology passes by. Monica Langer explains:

> In a very real sense, Merleau-Ponty's phenomenological description of perception starts from the everyday world of already acquired meanings and from the consciousness of an established, meaningful world. . . . The actual *birth* of meaning thus remains largely unexplored.[12]

According to Heidegger, human beings "stand outside" of themselves by taking over meaningful public patterns of comportment that are prescribed by "Anyone." There is no "I," no body-subject when describing the clearing of intelligibility. In my everyday activities, I am already being-with-others; I am "Anyone."

> *Proximally*, it is not "I," in the sense of my own self, that "am," but rather the Others, whose way is that of the "they." In terms of the "they" and as the "they," I am "given" proximally to "myself" [*mir "selbst"*]. Proximally Dasein is "they," and for the most part it remains so. . . . With this interpretation of being-with and being-one's self in the "they," the question of the "who" of everydayness of being-with-one-another is answered. (BT, 167)

The anonymous "Anyone" has not only decided in advance what roles, occupations, and norms I can take over but has also determined the meaning of my own embodied perceptions. My perceptions can only make sense to me if I am already familiar with a public context of intelligibility. For example, hearing as the perception of sounds is not primordially regarded as a pure sensation; rather, tones and sounds are already understood on the basis of a public clearing, allowing me to hear tones and sounds *as such*. Heidegger says, "What we *first* hear is never noises or complexes of sounds, but the creaking of a wagon, the motorcycle. We hear the column on the march, the north wind, the woodpecker tapping, the fire crackling" (BT, 207).

Third, Merleau-Ponty gives "primacy" to perception as the foundation for any meaningful experience whatsoever. There would be no world without perception.

> [Without] any perception of the whole we would not think
> of noticing the resemblance or the contiguity of its elements,
> but literally that they would not be part of the same world
> and would not exist at all. . . . All disclosure of the implicit
> and all cross-checking performed by perception vindicat-
> ed—in short, a realm of truth, a *world*. (PP, 16–17)

Although Merleau-Ponty is unclear on this point, there is a sense that
"cultural" meanings emerge out of the "natural" perceptual contact
between body and world, and that the layer of culture can somehow
be suspended or "bracketed" out in order to describe the structure of
perception.[13] Heidegger, on the other hand, points out that perception
is always already saturated with cultural meaning. Human beings are
socialized into a public network of relations, and it is on the basis of
these relations that perceptions make sense. The clearing of intelligibility is already laid out in advance, enabling me to hear the creaking
wagon or the din of the motorcycle. Thus embodied perception is
already determined by the "primacy" of Dasein. Without a shared
clearing that endows our perceptions with meaning and intelligibility,
all that I encounter are naked sounds and shapes.

   Fourth, because Merleau-Ponty's phenomenology focuses on the
prereflective perceptual connection that exists "now" between bodily
being and world, his project necessarily privileges the temporal dimension of the "present." All other dimensions of time are therefore seen
as being derived from the spontaneity characteristic of the present.

> *It is always in the present that we are centered, and our deci-*
> *sions start from there*; they can therefore always be brought
> into relationship with our past, and are never motiveless,
> and, though they may open up a cycle in our life which
> is entirely new, they still have to be subsequently carried
> forward. (PP, 427, emphasis added)

Merleau-Ponty privileges the temporality of the present because he
focuses exclusively on the nature of perception as the preobjective
starting point of all modes of comportment.

> *The solution of all problems of transcendence is to be sought in*
> *the thickness of the pre-objective present*, in which we find our
> bodily being, our social being, and the pre-existence of the
> world, that is, the starting point of "explanations," insofar
> as they are legitimate. (PP, 433, emphasis added)

Against this view, Heidegger argues that our comportment in the present is derived from and made possible by a more primordial temporal structure that cannot be understood in terms of perception. For Heidegger, any perception is already preshaped by the past *and* the future, by the temporal dimensions of "situatedness" (*Befindlich-keit*) and "projection" (*Entwurf*). Situatedness captures the sense that we are already *thrown* into a shared world, with a shared history, which reveals why things affect us in terms of specific dispositions or "moods" (*Stimmung*). Projection captures the sense in which our lives are already "on the way" (*unterwegs*) as we ceaselessly press forward into future possibilities that guide and define our identities.

In our everyday lives, we stretch backward, bringing our history with us as we move forward, engaging in various self-defining goals and projects, toward our ultimate possibility, death. For Heidegger, human existence is defined in terms of "thrown projection" (BT, 243), and it is only *on the basis of this* twofold movement that our bodily perceptions are intelligible and make sense to us. As the movement or happening of human life, time is not something that we "belong to" once we are born, as Merleau-Ponty suggests (PP, 140, 427). Rather, Dasein *is* temporality, and it is temporality that provides the scaffolding or frame of reference that makes it possible for things to emerge on the scene *as* the kinds of things that they are. Because Merleau-Ponty seeks to revive the living, prethematic bond between body-subject and worldly object, he overlooks the ontological fact that our present perceptions are rendered meaningful not by "incarnate consciousness" but by the a priori horizon of temporality.

In this regard, I want to suggest that Merleau-Ponty's phenomenology does not go far enough to overcome the assumptions of Cartesian subjectivity. In his later "Working Notes," Merleau-Ponty admits, "The problems posed in *Phenomenology of Perception* are insoluble because I start there from the 'consciousness' [subject]—'object' distinction" (VI, 233). By focusing on the perception, spatiality, and motility of incarnate consciousness, Merleau-Ponty is unable to give an account of the conditions for the possibility of meaning.[14] For Heidegger, Dasein, as the temporally structured clearing of intelligibility, is always already there, prior to the appearance of the body-subject.

Yet critics rightly point out that Heidegger's project becomes increasingly "formal," "neutral," and "abstract" as it withdraws and finally severs itself from what Heidegger refers to as the "ontical priority of Dasein," the concrete starting point for any fundamental ontology.[15] Heidegger confirms, "The results of the [existential] analysis show the peculiar *formality* and *emptiness* of any ontological determination" (BT,

292, emphases added). However, as his own Zollikon seminars suggest, this does not mean Heidegger is dismissing investigations into the problem of embodiment altogether. Indeed, clues in his lectures following *Being and Time* indicate that the existential analytic opens up the possibility of a "turn" (*Kehre*) back to the ontic aspects of Dasein, a turn now rooted in the "primal phenomenon of human existence itself" (MFL, 156). This return is not inconsistent with the position in *Being and Time*. For Heidegger, it is on the basis of the worldly, *existentiell* practices of ontic Dasein that any ontology "arises" and must eventually "return" (BT, 62).

The nature of this "turnaround" or "overturning" (*Umschlag*) is only briefly introduced in an appendix to his 1928 Leibniz lectures, where Heidegger distinguishes the "analytic of Dasein" from the "metaphysics of Dasein" (MFL, 157).[16] It is on the basis of the metaphysics of Dasein that philosophy can return to the specific anthropological and ethical aspects of existence that were passed over in the existential analytic.[17] In his 1929 lectures, entitled "Kant and the Problem of Metaphysics," Heidegger explains that the metaphysics of Dasein is nothing like a "fixed" conceptual system "about" a particular entity as, for example, "zoology is about animals." Rather, it is always transforming and being taken up anew, always working out the question of "what man is" (KPM, 162). Heidegger refers to this new investigation, which reexamines the concrete practices of ontic Dasein, as "metontology" (*Metontologie*).

I designate this set of questions *metontology*. And here also, in the domain of metontological-*existentiell* questioning, is the domain of the metaphysics of existence. (MFL, 157)

Metontology, or "metaphysical ontics" (*metaphysische Ontik*), is not a reference to the ontic investigations of the positive sciences.

[M]etontology is not a summary ontic in the sense of a general science that empirically assembles the results of the individual sciences into a so-called "world picture." (MFL, 157)

Metontology is associated with the ontic sciences only insofar as it has "beings as its subject matter." In short, Dasein is now thematized as *a* being, but not in terms of its static, present-at-hand attributes. Rather, it is thematized in terms of existence. Metontological-*existentiell* questioning, therefore, is already shaped by the results of the analytic of Dasein. It is for this reason that Heidegger suggests an essential union between fundamental ontology and metontology. "Metontology is possible," says Heidegger, "only on the basis and in the perspective of the radical ontological problematic and is possible conjointly with it" (MFL, 157).[18]

Based on the metontological view of the body, the assumptions of materialism and the positive sciences have been dismantled, and the body is no longer conceived as a bounded material entity that is separate and distinct from worldly objects. The body—now understood in terms of existence—is already at home, oriented in a concrete situation, prereflectively handling and manipulating a totality of beings. As an embodied agent, I am already familiar with a unified, pregiven background, and this embodied familiarity allows things—tools, signs, gestures, and events—to show up *as* the very things that they are. This means that body and world are not cut off from each other like subject and object. Rather, they always "belong together" in terms of Dasein (BP, 297).

At the end of *Being and Time*, Heidegger suggests that his own ontical starting point—which provides access to the question of the meaning of being—is only one possible path. "Whether this is the *only* way or even the right one at all," says Heidegger, "can be decided *only after one has gone along it*" (BT, 487). Heidegger, therefore, recognizes that his path is "limited," and it will invariably neglect certain factical aspects of existence (BT, 38). These aspects can be taken up again by metontology, by the metaphysics of Dasein. And philosophy will inevitably return to the concerns of metontology, because the existential analytic is itself made possible by a metaphysics of finite historical existence.[19] Indeed, as Heidegger says in 1929, fundamental ontology is only "the first level" of the metaphysics of Dasein.

> The metaphysics of Dasein, guided by the question of ground-laying, should unveil the ontological constitution of [Dasein] in such a way that it proves to be that which makes possible [the *existentiell*]. . . . Fundamental ontology is only the first level of the metaphysics of Dasein. What belongs to this [metaphysics of Dasein] *as a whole*, and how from time to time it is rooted historically in factical Dasein, cannot be discussed here." (KPM, 162–63)

It can be argued that this theme endures in Heidegger. As late as his 1962 lecture, "On Time and Being," Heidegger expressed the importance of repeating an analysis of the ontic aspects of Dasein after the "meaning of being had been clarified," features that the positive sciences were never able to grasp and thus had to be taken up in a "completely different way" (OTB, 32).

With the conception of metontology in place, we can now turn our attention to the possibility that the world constructs ontic Dasein in terms of a particular gendered identity, an identity that shapes our everyday understanding of things. Feminist critics, in this regard, have attempted to give flesh to Heidegger's admittedly "abstract" and "neutral" account of embodied agency by exploring the possibility of a gendered incarnation of Dasein and by identifying the ways in which the world may already be structured around hierarchical and exclusionary discursive practices.

Gender and Time

On the Question of Dasein's Neutrality

Initially it may seem strange to engage Heidegger from the standpoint of feminist theory, because his meditations on the meaning of being are far removed from the ontic concerns of social, political, and ethical philosophy. However, as we have seen, Heidegger's approach to the question of being begins with his own *existentiell* interpretation of ordinary, concrete life. Heidegger's departure from a conception of understanding based on detached theorizing in favor of everyday social understanding would appear to make him attractive to the concerns of feminist theory.[1] And, beginning in the early 1980s,[2] feminist philosophy has provided significant contributions and criticisms particularly regarding the lack of bodily concreteness and gender specificity in Heidegger's analysis of everyday life.[3]

Again, Heidegger avoids a thematic discussion of the body by focusing on the structures for any meaningful bodily experience whatsoever. According to Heidegger, we dwell in these structures of meaning by virtue of our being-in-the-world, and these structures are "asexual" (*geschlechtslos*) or "neutral" (*neutrale*) because they are more original than the particular biological characteristics of "man" or "woman." But what Heidegger does not appear to recognize is that our concrete acts and practices have a certain gender identity that is socially constructed and historically constituted, an identity that is already marked by masculinity, already privileging a particular set of habits, institutions, and languages. The question we come to is this: Is Heidegger's project shortsighted because it fails to grasp the fact that the disclosive clearing we rely on to interpret things as such is already ordered in terms of oppressive social hierarchies?

Fundamental Ontology and the Sex/Gender Divide

In the wake of Gayle Rubin's pioneering 1975 essay, "The Traffic in Women," English-speaking feminist philosophers have, for the most part, appropriated the distinction between "sex" and "gender."[4] Sex has come to be understood as a reference to the fixed, unchanging biological parts of "man" and "woman." Gender, on the other hand, refers to the culturally constructed norms and practices that are interpreted as "masculine" and "feminine." The category of sex usually brings with it an "essentialist" universal point of reference insofar as the biological body provides an invariable ground, and the category of gender is usually regarded as "antiessentialist" because social practices are not fixed and permanent; they are determined by the dynamic changes and events of history. To this end, feminist philosophers have largely rejected the determinist assumption that biological differences between the sexes justify differences in social norms. The problem of oppression, based on the feminist view, is not biological; rather, it is a product of specific, historically shaped social norms, practices, and institutions. In short, it is a problem of gender.[5] Where does the sex/ gender distinction fit into Heidegger's conception of human existence, understood as Dasein?

Heidegger's unwillingness to talk about Dasein's sexual nature is understandable, given his attempt to dismantle the tradition of substance ontology. As we saw earlier, the interpretation of substance that shows up today in mainstream Anglophone philosophy is largely understood in terms of materialism. According to Heidegger, giving an account of the material body, the anatomical "what-ness" of human beings, is not crucial for the analytic of Dasein, because such an account fails to ask about the "to be," the unique way in which human beings concretely exist in the world. Interpreting what is essential to human existence in terms of the material characteristics of sex would continue to treat the being (*Sein*) of humans as *a* being (*Seiende*). For Heidegger, Dasein is, first and foremost, not *a* static entity that is physically present but a dynamic "way of being," an ongoing, finite movement *on the basis of which* we come to understand and make sense of intraworldly entities, including ourselves.

To this end, Heidegger suggests that it is misguided to regard Dasein as a corporeal thing, as a sexed "man" or "woman" with biological properties that can be theoretically examined (BT, 79). Heidegger wants to return to the ordinary activity of human existence itself that underlies and makes possible any and all objective theorizing. In the flow of our everyday lives, there is no detached, theoretical awareness of objects. We are, rather, already engaged in a public world, and any theoretical awareness of things presupposes a tacit familiarity with this world. At this point, we can draw some initial conclusions concerning the relationship between Heidegger's early writings and the sex/gender distinction.

Because Heidegger's project undermines traditional substance ontology, it is critical toward the essentialist category "sex." For Heidegger, human beings should not be interpreted fundamentally in terms of the fixed objective "presence" (*Anwesenheit*) of body parts. Rather, the dynamic "to be" of human existence is more appropriately understood under the category "gender," which captures the way our ongoing self-interpreting practices are socially and culturally constructed. However, for Heidegger, the *Da*, the shared space of meaning, should be regarded as asexual or neutral, because it is already "there," prior to interpreting ourselves in terms of our gendered practices or anatomical characteristics. In his 1928 Marburg lectures on Leibniz, Heidegger says:

> The term "man" was not used for that being which is the theme of the analysis. Instead, the neutral term *Dasein* was chosen. . . . This neutrality also indicates that Dasein is neither of the two sexes. (MFL, 136)

Yet in his "Introduction to Philosophy," a series of Freiburg lectures during the winter semester of 1928–29, Heidegger claims that Dasein's neutrality is "broken" (*gebrochen*) insofar as it exists factically.

> In its essence, the entity that we are is something neutral (*ein Neutrum*). We call this entity Dasein. However, it belongs to the essence of this neutral being that, insofar as it exists factically, it has necessarily broken its neutrality, that is, Dasein as factical is either masculine or feminine; it is a sexual [gendered] creature (*Geschlechtswesen*). (IP, 146)

This tension between "gendered" and "neutral" Dasein can be grasped only if we revisit the methodology and motivation of Heidegger's early project.

Gendered Dasein and Neutral Da-sein

Again, *Being and Time* is an attempt at fundamental ontology, a mode of investigation concerned with unearthing the structures that allow beings to emerge-into-presence in their being. These structures can only be discovered when we pay careful attention to and describe the way phenomena initially show up in our everyday practices, prior to any theoretical assumptions. At this level of phenomenological description, Dasein is, in each case, masculine or feminine; it is, as Heidegger says, "a gendered creature." As a man, Heidegger's starting point has a specific gender identity based on a particular masculine understanding of being. This understanding is embodied in the everyday social acts and practices of an early twentieth-century German male who also happens to be young, educated, middle class, and relatively healthy.[6] Because his *existentiell* descriptions are already shaped by a background of patriarchal social norms, it is obviously not self-evident to Heidegger that he must announce his own gender identity in *Being and Time*. As Simone de Beauvoir reminds us, as a man he does not have to.[7] "A man never begins by affirming that he is an individual of a certain sex; that he is a man goes without saying."[8] What is important for our purposes, however, is that the *existentiell* inquiry into his own particular ways of being must be distinguished from the existential inquiry into the essential structures of any understanding of being—whether masculine, feminine, or otherwise—whatsoever. This distinction needs to be fully explained.

Although it may not have been made explicit until 1928–29, Heidegger's characterization of Dasein implies two different but interrelated formulations. First, Dasein is to be interpreted as a factical, ontic entity that embodies the activity of existing. Each individual man or woman is an instantiation of Dasein, because our own *existentiell* engagements are disclosive insofar as we embody specific social practices that are already colored with worldly "significance" (*Bedeutsamkeit*). By taking over, for instance, the traditional roles of the responsible working father or the caring mother and housewife, human beings individually produce meaning; we bring things into a clearing, into a meaningful public space. Thus "[factical] Dasein brings its 'there' along with it. If it lacks its 'there,' it is not factically the entity which is essentially Dasein" (BT, 171).

Second, Dasein is to be interpreted as *the* Da-sein, as the "being of the-there." The emphasis here is not on the particular concrete engagements of the individual but on the "there" as the disclosive field or "openness" that lets beings show up in their being. In this case, Da-sein is understood as the "clearing" or "there" that springs from and is sustained by social acts and practices.[9] If my own social practices "clear," then I participate in maintaining the clearing; I am "being-its-there." "As being-in-the-world, [Dasein] is cleared [*gelichtet*] in itself," says Heidegger, "not through any other being, but in such a way that it *is* itself the clearing" (BT, 171).

Fundamental ontology, therefore, begins with phenomenological descriptions of the *existentiell* engagements of ontic Dasein understood in the first sense, where "Dasein as factical is either masculine or feminine." The goal of this inquiry, however, is to arrive at the neutral—ontological-existential—structures of *the* Da-sein, understood in the second sense. We can say, therefore, that the neutrality of Dasein is "broken" insofar as we are each gendered, factical beings, however, it is only *on the basis of* Da-sein's structural neutrality that any human being can make sense of her or his life. Heidegger explains:

> The broken neutrality belongs to the essence of humans; that means, however, that this essence can become a problem only on the basis of neutrality, and the breakup of neutrality is itself possible only in relation to this neutrality. In this problem, sexuality is only a moment and, indeed, not the primary moment. (IP, 147)

As we saw in chapter 1, beginning the existential analytic by describing one's own *existentiell* interpretation of things, whether "masculine" or "feminine," is problematic, precisely because one's own interpretation of everyday life is a "misinterpretation" due to the fact that it is invariably guided by the assumptions and prejudices of the social world within which one is thrown. This means there is no Archimedean ground from which the structures of understanding become transparent. However, just because Heidegger's phenomenological starting point is shot through with the contingency and arbitrariness of patriarchal assumptions does not mean that he is espousing a version of historicism. Heidegger's goal is to "press on" beyond the culturally specific projects of "man" or "woman" to the invariable structures that make it possible for any human being to make sense of the world.

What is important to recognize at this point is that the structural conditions that constitute Dasein are, according to Heidegger, asexual or neutral. Dasein, as an open space of meaning, is not only prior to the particular characteristics and practices of individual human beings. Dasein already guides any interpretation that we can have of the world, making it possible for things to show up *as* masculine or feminine in the first place. However, a deeper problem remains that involves the structure of Dasein itself.

If we make sense of things only in terms of the "there," understood as a historically mediated background of social acts and practices, then it can be argued that this background itself is already marked by masculinity, already privileging a particular set of habits, institutions, and languages. The question we come to is this: Is Heidegger's project shortsighted because it fails to grasp the fact that the disclosive clearing we rely upon to interpret things *as such* is ordered in terms of gendered hierarchies? This criticism is particularly sharp if we maintain—as many Heidegger commentators do—that the origin or source of meaning is "the Anyone" (*das Man*).

Again, "meaning" (*Sinn*) is not generated by the mental activity of a self-enclosed consciousness but emerges from the shared world in which we are involved. Heidegger is stressing the fact that our understanding of things is public. I am engaged in the acts and practices that "they" are engaged in, and "they" assign meaning and value to my life. *Das Man*, as an interconnected nexus of social relations, determines in advance the possible ways I can understand or interpret the world. *Das Man*, therefore, accompanies me in all of my various concrete engagements with things.

Feminist critics, for the most part, agree with Heidegger's position, that the interpretation or understanding we have of ourselves is not determined by essential biological differences but by the sociohistorical situation into which we are thrown. Yet they are simultaneously critical of Heidegger because he says nothing about the ways in which this social situation is hierarchical and exclusionary. If we recognize that *das Man* indelibly shapes the way we interpret ourselves as either man or woman, then we must also recognize that the meaningful social roles and practices we grow into are uniquely patriarchal. They embody a very specific kind of "inhibiting, confining, and objectifying" social domination. As Iris Marion Young says:

> The modalities of feminine bodily comportment . . . have their source [in] neither anatomy nor physiology, and certainly not in a mysterious feminine essence. Rather, they have their source in the particular *situation* of women as conditioned by their sexist oppression in contemporary society. . . . Insofar as we learn to live out our existence in accordance with the definition that patriarchal culture assigns to us, we are physically inhibited, confined, positioned, and objectified.[10]

In short, feminist criticisms can bring to light how Heidegger's project overlooks the fact that public patterns of gendered domination are an essential part of *das Man*.

According to this criticism, it is precisely because the world is rendered intelligible on the basis of *das Man* that it is correct to say that Dasein is not neutral but gendered in terms of a patriarchal order. It is by means of a gendered clearing that the "woman" has traditionally come to interpret herself as inferior, a "fragile thing [to be] *looked at and acted upon*."[11] Again, if *das Man* is the locus of meaning, "governing" the possible ways we make sense of things, and if *das Man* privileges masculine practices and discourse and distorts and suppresses those that are nonmasculine, then it is appropriate to say that Dasein *is* gendered.

Furthermore, conceiving of Dasein in terms of neutrality is problematic, because it has a tendency to "equalize" the sexes; it makes humans the same, sexless, and it ignores difference. More specifically, it fails to recognize uniquely feminine modes of disclosure that may have been subsumed and compartmentalized under a patriarchal space of meaning. Luce Irigaray, in this regard, suggests that the woman is simply "reproduced" by the Western clearing *as* nonmasculine, irrational, emotional, and so forth. In this sense, the very conception of sexual equality can be construed as a danger to feminist thought because it conceals sexual difference (SG, 115).

Following Irigaray's lead, Tina Chanter has pointed out that the woman's unique understanding of being suffers from a "double burden" in the West. First, bodily desires and needs, traditionally associated with the feminine, are largely ignored by the philosophical tradition, because they are irrelevant or counterproductive to the disembodied, rational pursuit of universal truths. Second, the brief history of the feminist movement again ignores the embodied reality of the woman by seeking social and political equality with men.[12] Hence, the feminist cry for equality is problematic, because it continues to overlook the unique alterity of feminine modes of disclosure; it forgets sexual difference, that there are *other* understandings of being, *other* ways for beings to show up. Irigaray explains:

> If the female gender does not make a demand, all too often it is based upon a claim for equal rights and this risks ending in the destruction of gender. . . . But [this happens] if the self is equal to *one* and not to *two*, if it comes down to sameness and to split in *sameness* and ignores the other *as* other. (SG, 115)

Based on this view, if our shared historical language is to be regarded as "the lighting/concealing advent of being itself," as Heidegger suggests (LH, 206), then this advent is already rooted in sexual difference. It is a language that excludes and denies the embodied reality of the feminine and in turn determines the being of beings, where beings show up only in terms of certain restrictions and silences. Irigaray writes:

> The language of . . . patriarchal culture [has] reduced the value of the feminine to such a degree that their reality and their description of the world are incorrect. Thus, instead of remaining a different gender, the feminine has become, in our language, the non-masculine, that is to say abstract nonexistent reality. . . . [It] defines her as an object in relation to the male subject. This accounts for the fact that women find it so difficult to speak and to be heard as women. They are excluded and denied by the patriarchal order. They cannot be women and speak in a sensible, coherent manner. (JTN, 20)

Irigaray agrees with Heidegger that language is the disclosive "saying" of history; however, this historical saying is not sexless; it is inscribed with *"men's discourse,"* one that designates reality as an "always already cultural reality, linked to the individual and collective history of the masculine subject" (JTN, 35). Irigaray contends that the domination of patriarchal language in the West has forced women to "speak the same language as [men]," and that this domination has been pervasive since "the time of the Greeks" (SWN, 25). While supporting Heidegger's conception of an authentic historical "retrieval" that recovers the primordial wellsprings or origins of our current understanding of being, Irigaray maintains that Heidegger's retrieval fails to go deep enough because it stops at the commencement of patriarchal history born in fifth-century Greek philosophy.

Irigaray's genealogical retrieval seeks to unearth an ancient maternal language that predates the origins of Attic Greek civilization. "[She] would have to dig down very deep to discover the traces of this civilization, of this history, the vestiges of a more archaic civilization that might give some clue to woman's sexuality. This extremely ancient civilization would undoubtedly have a different alphabet, a different language" (SWN, 25). This recovery would reconnect our understanding of being with the wellsprings of a maternal language that has long been forgotten.[13]

This criticism of Heidegger holds insofar as there is agreement concerning *das Man* as the origin of intelligibility. In other words, it is only on the basis of "the Anyone"—understood as a background of linguistic practices—that human beings can make sense of things. However, to reduce the origin of meaning to a context of discursive practices is to overlook the fundamental insight of Heidegger's early project, namely, that "temporality" (*Zeitlichkeit*) is the ultimate origin of meaning. And the horizon of temporality is neutral because it is both constitutive of and ontologically prior to *das Man*.[14]

The Gender and Neutrality of Time

There is strong evidence in Heidegger to support the claim that the discursive practices of *das Man* serve as the condition for the possibility of meaning, and the most influential proponent of this view is undoubtedly Hubert Dreyfus, who says:

> For Heidegger . . . the source of the intelligibility of the world is the average public practices through which alone there can be any understanding at all. What is shared is not a conceptual scheme, . . . [but] simply our average comportment. Once a practice has been explained by appealing to what one does, no more basic explanation is possible. . . . [T]he constant control *das Man* exerts over each Dasein makes a coherent referential whole, shared for-the-sake-of-whichs, and thus, ultimately, significance and intelligibility possible.[15]

Das Man is certainly an existential structure of Dasein. As Heidegger says, "The self of everyday Dasein is the they-self. . . . [And] as they-self, the particular Dasein has been dispersed into the 'they,' and must find itself" (BT, 167). But it is not only a structure. It also appears to represent *the* entire "context of significance," the source of meaning and intelligibility for each factical Dasein.

> Dasein is for the sake of the "they" in an everyday manner, and the "they" itself articulates the referential context of significance. (BT, 167)

My individual activities are meaningful because I am an embodiment of *das Man*. I am a crossing point in a public nexus of intelligibility, a nexus that was already there, prior to my own emergence on the scene.[16]

The meaning-giving capacity of our everyday social relations is undeniable. However, interpreting *das Man* as the ultimate determination for intelligibility is not consistent with the argument of *Being and*

Time. For Heidegger, *das Man* is to be regarded as only one of a number of equiprimordial structures of Dasein, structures such as "situatedness" (*Befindlichkeit*), "understanding" (*Verstehen*), "falling" (*Verfallen*), and "discourse" (*Rede*), which are all equally necessary and essential conditions of Dasein. Furthermore, as Pierre Keller and David Weberman point out, even if this interpretation of *das Man* does articulate the shared nexus of intelligibility, it fails to ask: "What makes possible this sharable making sense of the world in the first place?"[17]

Again, fundamental ontology begins with phenomenological descriptions of factical Dasein as she or he is concretely engaged in the world. The aim of this ontic-*existentiell* inquiry is to uncover the essential structures that constitute the shared clearing of intelligibility. Yet this uncovering is "provisional" or "preparatory" until we arrive at "temporality" as the original "horizon for all understanding of being and for any way of interpreting it" (BT, 39). The results of this deeper inquiry, as we saw in chapter 1, reveal that temporality is the meaning of being of Dasein itself.

For Heidegger, Dasein must ultimately be understood in terms of temporality, as the twofold movement of "thrown projection," which represents the frame of reference *on the basis of which* things can light up as intelligible or remain dark and unintelligible. "Ecstatic temporality," says Heidegger, "originally lights/clears (*lichtet*) the there" (BT, 402). This temporal framework is referred to as "Care" (*Sorge*), an expression that represents the basic ground of intelligibility, a ground that is prior to *das Man* and is constituted by the fact that Dasein is always "ahead-of-itself-already-in-(the-world) as being-alongside (entities encountered within-the-world)" (BT, 237).[18] Again, Dasein is not a being that moves along *in* time. Rather, Dasein—as an already opened clearing of intelligibility—*is* time.[19]

For some critics, Heidegger's account of "primordial temporality" remains problematic, because it diminishes the importance of the temporal *ec-stasis* of the "Present" (*Gegenwart*). For Heidegger, the being of beings is preshaped by the ecstasies of "Past" (*Gewesenheit*) and "Future" (*Zukunft*); these are the essential structures that make up the "there" that allows things to emerge-into-presence *as* the kinds of things that they are.

Looking at Heidegger's 1924 Marburg lecture, "The Concept of Time," and his Kassel lecture of 1925 is particularly helpful, because it is here that Heidegger begins to outline the account of temporality that will emerge in *Being and Time*. In these lectures, Heidegger refers to Dasein's existence as fundamentally futural, an anticipatory "running forward" toward shared possibilities, projects, and roles "which

I am not yet, but will be" (DHW, 169).[20] It is by existing or "running forward" that Dasein circles back on the past, appropriating the beliefs, acts, and practices of the shared world within which she or he is thrown. This circling back allows things to meaningfully count and matter for Dasein in one way or another. To this end, "acting in the direction of the future, [lets] the past come alive" (DHW, 169). This twofold movement determines the horizon within which beings can come into play, and the temporal moment of the present is already rooted in this stretching forward "towards itself" and "back to" the past. Indeed, from the perspective of primordial temporality, "the present vanishes" altogether (DHW, 169).

Heidegger downplays the role of the present, because it has a tendency to "break away" or dominate the other ecstasies insofar as we become "absorbed" and "lost" in the now, in the mundane, conformist affairs of "the Anyone." Heidegger refers to everyday "making present" as an "indifferent" way of being, which is tantamount to being "inauthentic." Inauthentic life is busy with things, whereby we always remain "curious" and "fascinated" with the outer appearances of things, without attempting to understand where this curiosity comes from or where it is heading. To this end, the present dominates us insofar as we invariably get caught up in "publicness," in the latest social fads and fashions, in the material commodities and public roles that we cling to for a source of security and comfort. As a result, in our everyday dealings, we are inevitably pulled into what Heidegger calls "the movement of falling" (BT, 264). It is by this entanglement with the present that Dasein flees from authenticity, refusing to face the mood of anxiety, the mood that disrupts our engagement in everyday affairs. Anxiety makes it possible for us to resolutely own up to the unsettledness of our existence, an unsettledness structured by the very movement of time as "thrown projection" itself. Absorbed in everyday affairs, we have a tendency to "leap away from [our] authentic future and from [our] authentic having been" (BT, 348).

Of course, as John Caputo and others have pointed out, Heidegger's own conception of "resoluteness" (*Entschlossenheit*) is not neutral; it is gendered to the extent that is marked by masculinity. Authentic Dasein emerges as manly, like a soldier, ready for the "struggle" (*Kampf*), ready to face the contingency of existence alone, heroic and unbending. The possibility of a bodily response to anxiety, of breaking down and weeping, is unrecognized. Caputo writes:

> The "fundamental ontology" of Dasein, which was supposed to occupy a place of a priori neutrality, prior to the division

between the genders, is deeply marked and inscribed by the
traits of a very masculine subject, a knight of anticipatory
resoluteness, ready for anxiety, a macho, virile figure out
there all alone "without its mommy," as Drucilla Cornell
once quipped.[21]

An alternative to this stoic brand of authenticity may be one that is
rooted in the body, a body that *feels* the black mood of anxiety, feels
withdrawn from the stability of everyday social routines. The response
to anxiety, in this case, may be to cry, to reach out to others, to talk
or touch, a response grounded in the understanding that we are, in
our everyday lives, more than conformist automatons that constantly
flee from death. In the present, we are also sensual, empathic, desir-
ing beings.

    As we saw earlier, Merleau-Ponty offered one of the first chal-
lenges to Heidegger's conception of temporality by suggesting that the
past and the future are actually derived from the spontaneity of the
living present, insofar as the present represents our original sensual
contact with the world, the preobjective starting point of all modes of
comportment. According to Merleau-Ponty, Heidegger forgets that "it
is always in the present that we are centered and our decisions start
from there" (PP, 433). Many commentators expand on Merleau-Ponty's
criticism, arguing that Heidegger's interpretation of temporality is too
narrow because it reduces our involvement in everyday affairs to a
form of workaday inauthenticity.

    For instance, Chanter argues that it is because Heidegger makes
"no effort to produce a positive experiential account of the lived
body ... [that he] neglects what most would regard as important
aspects of experience, for example, sexuality, eroticism, enjoyment,
and pleasure, or, at best treats them as only important as subordinate
to successful negotiation of equipment relations."[22] Indeed, the entire
dimension of the present embodied in experiences of desire, love, or
pleasure is missing in Heidegger's account of everydayness. For Heidegger, it appears that we would no longer *exist* if we lingered in the
present to enjoy sensual pleasures, appreciating a sunset or a landscape,
listening to music, or sharing a bottle of wine with a friend.[23] This is
because in these sensual activities I am not "doing" anything.

    Karl Löwith recalls Heidegger's preoccupation with practical
action by describing his disgust with the "idleness" of summer vaca-
tioners in the Black Forest.

    [In Heidegger] there follows a polemical invective directed
    against the edified "city-dwellers" who come to the Black

Forest during their vacations in order to "examine" and
"enjoy" its beauty in an objective manner—two words
which have a despicable ring for Heidegger, because they
indicate idle behavior lacking in "action." [He says that]
he himself never "examines" the landscape; instead it is
his "work world."[24]

Based on this view, it appears that Heidegger regards the world
primarily as a "system of tools" and forgets the simple fact that the
body first needs to enjoy nourishment and rest in order to handle the
tools of the "work-world." Emmanuel Levinas explains:

What seems to have escaped Heidegger—if it is true that in
these matters something might have escaped Heidegger—is
that prior to being a system of tools the world is an ensemble
of nourishments. Human life in the world does not go
beyond the objects that fulfill it. It is perhaps not correct
to say that we live to eat, but it is not more correct to say
that we eat to live.[25]

Levinas suggests that the pleasure of sharing a meal with friends is
irrelevant for Heidegger; the meal should be understood primarily as
"fuel" for the purposive activities of the laborer.

[Heidegger's] world as a set of implements forming a system
and suspended on the care of an existence anxious for its
being interpreted as an onto-logy, attests labor, habitation,
the home, and economy; but in addition, it bears witness
to a particular organization of labor in which "foods" take
on the signification of fuel in the economic machinery. *It is
interesting to observe that Heidegger does not take the relation
of enjoyment into consideration.* The implement has entirely
masked the usage and the issuance of the term—satisfaction. Dasein in Heidegger is never hungry. Food can be
interpreted only in a world of exploitation.[26]

The emphasis that Heidegger places on the present as a mode of
being rooted in conformist, workaday comportment not only neglects
basic bodily needs such as eating and sleeping, but it overlooks the
significance of felt, face-to-face relations in our everyday lives: of the
arguments between husband and wife or the attentiveness of the mother
for her child. By focusing on the instrumental dealings of the work
world and ignoring the joyful, painful, emotional dimensions of the

present, Heidegger presents a familiar theme in Western thought, one that refuses to recognize the sources of embodied desire, emotionality, and sexuality that give voice to the feminine. Thus regardless of his attempt to overcome metaphysics by emphasizing the priority of practical involvement over detached theorizing, Heidegger's interpretation of the present as a fallen mode of time may situate his thought squarely within a traditional prejudice.[27]

Although there is certainly force to these observations, they do not fundamentally undermine Heidegger's project. In the case of the embodied experience of "empathy" (*Einfühlung*), for example, Heidegger will argue that it is only because the other has already been disclosed *as such—as* a daughter, a wife, a friend, or simply another human being—that we can, in the present, feel affection for them. Again, fundamental ontology is primarily concerned with the conditions that make the world meaningful, allowing things to show up *as* such and such. And it is *not* by my present involvement in the world that things make sense to me. The world is meaningful because as I invariably press forward into social possibilities, I am thrown back into a public situation where things already count and matter to me. It is only *on the basis of* this horizon of "thrown projection" that I can interpret myself and the world in one way or another. To this end, empathy does not reveal a "primordial existential structure," because the experience of empathy is always mediated in advance by a temporally structured familiarity with the other; the other, to some extent, already matters and makes sense to me. Thus for Heidegger, individual experiences such as empathy are themselves made possible by Dasein (BT, 161–63).

This, of course, does not mean that Heidegger's critique of the present is irrelevant to the concerns of feminist theory. If, as Judith Butler says, "feminist theory seeks to dislodge sexuality from those reifying ideologies which freeze sexual relations into forms of domination," then Heidegger's account of temporality has significant potential.[28] Earlier we saw how our everyday involvement in the world results in a presence-oriented perspective that increasingly determines our understanding of being. The consequence, for Heidegger, is that the temporal dimension of the present tempts us to turn away from an authentic awareness of our own contingent situatedness and finite possibilities. Caught up in the present, we have a tendency to hold onto the assumptions and prejudices of our tradition, a tradition that continues to maintain the metaphysics of hierarchical binaries, where the domination of "man" over "woman" shows up in terms of constant presence. This is because the present offers a horizon that is confined to beings, to the fixed and homogeneous characteristics of what-is. Such a horizon fails to recognize the abyssal structure of time. Specifically, it overlooks the movement of Dasein's thrown-finitude, a movement that simultaneously stretches backward toward its irretrievable past and forward toward possibilities that are "not yet."

For Heidegger, primordial temporality is a groundless, abysmal ground. As such, it holds open the possibilities for other horizons that are not trapped in the metaphysics of presence. In light of feminist concerns, the ecstasies of past and future contain the possibility of freeing thinking from essentialism, letting what has been absent in our own patriarchal tradition emerge out of concealment. Heidegger's notion of the authentic recovery of these ecstasies can be appropriated by feminist philosophers insofar as it may open new social horizons that allow a "reworking of gender binaries" so that one does not continue to stifle and dominate the other.[29] This is because, for Heidegger, thinking always has the possibility of emancipating itself from fallenness, thereby disrupting the oppressive hierarchies that have taken hold in our everyday practices.

Indeed, there is suggestive evidence in Heidegger that his goal of recovering the enigmatic question of being—by phenomenological attentiveness to everyday life—already resonates to core concerns in feminist philosophy. Carol Bigwood, for instance, reminds us that there is a woman, a Thracian maid, who can be interpreted as playing a small but important role in Heidegger's conception of recovery. The example comes about in the winter semester of 1935–36, during a lecture entitled "Basic Questions of Metaphysics." In this lecture, Heidegger suggests returning to a story told by Plato in the *Theaetetus*.

> The story is that Thales, while occupied in studying the heaven above and looking up, fell into a well. A good-looking and whimsical maid from Thrace laughed at him and told him that while he might passionately want to know all things in the universe, the things in front of his very nose and feet were unseen. (WIT, 3)

Heidegger continues, "[We] shall do well to remember occasionally that by our [philosophical] strolling we can fall into a well whereby we may not reach ground for some time" (WIT, 3).

These remarks can be appropriated by feminist philosophy because they reveal the failure of Thales' detached theorizing to grasp the original appearing or self-showing of things, the "things-thinging." In order to do this, we must pay attention to concrete embodied experience, to what is right "under our nose," to what is "near" and "by the hand." The Thracian maid, on this reading, teaches us something that the disembodied perspective of the Western tradition cannot, namely, to be attentive to what the body immediately feels and perceives. Heidegger explains:

> As we ask "What is a thing?" we now mean the things around us. We take in view what is most immediate, most capably of being grasped by the hand. By observing such, we reveal that we have learned something from the laughter of the housemaid. She thinks we should first look around thoroughly in this round-about-us (*Um-uns-herum*). (WIT, 7)

Bigwood interprets the handmaid's laughter in the face of the great Thales as an act of feminine wisdom, rebellion, and power that has, like so many examples from pre-Socratic Greece, been forgotten.[30]

The problem with the example of the Thracian maid is that it appears to perpetuate hierarchical oppositions based on the separation of gender roles. The woman is a maid trapped in domestic labor, carrying water from the well and watching her feet as she walks on the cobblestone. The man is involved in abstract, intellectual labor, freed from the duties of house and home. If one of the goals of Heidegger's project is to undermine the tradition of bifurcated metaphysics, then we should try to find an example that blurs the notion of gender identity, where, for instance, the man thinks, writes, and lives like a woman. Interestingly, Heidegger provides an example of this when he tells the story of Heraclitus in his "Letter on Humanism."

In this story, a group of foreign tourists has traveled to Heraclitus's home in an attempt to catch a glimpse of the great philosopher in a moment of deep thought. Instead, they find Heraclitus in the kitchen, preparing dinner and warming himself by the stove. The tourists are disappointed to see the philosopher involved in such a mundane domestic activity. They are on the verge of leaving, when Heraclitus, realizing their frustration, invites them all to come into the kitchen with the words "Here too the gods are present" (LH, 256–57). With this example, the separation of social roles based on sexual difference breaks down. Heraclitus is not being "manly." He is doing what the woman does; he is tending to his abode, his dwelling place, his hearth and home, and, in so doing, he recognizes that he stands in "the open region for the presencing of god" (LH, 258). Heraclitus, like the Thracian maid, is paying attention to ordinary places, preserving what is "near." To this end, both are being "ethical" by caring for and protecting the "abode," the concrete "dwelling place," of humans (LH, 233–35). Perhaps the Thracian maid and Heraclitus embody what Heidegger will call the *other* way of being, one that does not force beings into binary categories but patiently "lets" (*lassen*) beings emerge, ripen, and flourish on their own terms. We will return to this theme of "releasement" or "letting beings be" (*Gelassenheit*) in chapter 6, but at this point we need to situate this discussion of gender identity within the context of Heidegger's overall project.

As we saw earlier, to focus on concrete practices, whether masculine or feminine, is not essential to the program of fundamental ontology. It is only because we dwell in a shared, temporally structured space of meaning that we can engage in and make sense of embodied experiences. The space of meaning, in this regard, is always prior to—indeed, it is the condition for—any sociopolitical hierarchies that emerge in everyday life. Heidegger's project is not overly concerned with identifying all of the possible ways in which human beings are involved with things and others in everydayness. This would require endless provisional investigations into factical existence. Rather, the existential analytic seeks the general conditions that allow beings to initially emerge-into-presence in their being. For Heidegger, temporality grounds all of the particular *existentiell* modifications of concrete living, whether authentic or inauthentic—including those shaped by the specificities of sex, gender, ethnicity, age, disability, and so forth.

We can say, therefore, that temporality is the "primal source" of any intelligibility, any concrete possibility whatsoever, whether it is the factical practices of an individual man or woman or the patriarchal nexus of *das Man*. Heidegger confirms this point in 1928 when he writes, "Temporality is nothing other than the temporal condition for the possibility of world" (MFL, 208). Indeed, for Heidegger, the horizon of temporality is neutral concerning gender, precisely because it is prior to and makes possible an understanding of sexual difference.

> Neutrality is not the voidness of an abstraction, but precisely the potency of the origin, which bears in itself the intrinsic possibility of every concrete factual humanity. . . . Neutral Dasein is indeed the primal source of intrinsic possibility that springs up in every existence and makes it intrinsically possible. (MFL, 137)

This finally takes us back to Derrida's criticism of Heidegger in his first *Geschlecht* essay in 1983, "*Geschlecht*: Sexual Difference, Ontological

Difference."[31] In this essay, Derrida claims that Heidegger's interpretation of Dasein's "neutrality" simply reinstalls a familiar metaphysical binary, one that remains hierarchical, in the sense that Dasein's formal neutrality is more primordial than embodied sexual difference. Derrida suggests that Heidegger's neutral conception of Dasein is not asexual; it is entrenched in a "pre-differentiated," "pre-dual" sexuality.

> Whether a matter of neutrality or asexuality, the words accentuate strongly a negativity. . . . If Dasein as such belongs to neither of the two sexes, that doesn't mean that it is deprived of sex. On the contrary, here one must think of a pre-differential, rather a pre-dual, sexuality—which doesn't necessarily mean unitary, homogenous or undifferentiated. Then, from that sexuality, more originary than the dyad, one may try to think to the bottom a "positivity" and a "power." (G1, 60)

Heidegger's reading of sexual difference as inessential or nonprimordial, therefore, "is a schema we have recognized before," insofar as Dasein is ultimately interpreted in terms of disembodied formal structures, a source of original sexless purity (G1, 70). This repeats a common theme in the West from Plato to Kant, one that continues to downplay the importance of the body in general and sexual difference in particular. For Derrida, the removal of *Geschlecht* from the essential structures of Dasein *"confirms all the most traditional philosophemes, repeating them with force of a new rigor"* (G1, 68, emphases added).

Yet we now see that Derrida's criticism is only partially correct. Heidegger certainly does acknowledge the role of sexual difference, recognizing Dasein as a gendered creature. Dasein is, after all, "in each case mine" (*Jemeinigkeit*). In order to gain access to the question of the meaning of being, fundamental ontology must begin with the hermeneutic of ontic Dasein. It is from this ontical starting point that any philosophy "arises" and must eventually "return."[32] In short, all philosophy must begin with an interpretation offered by a finite, historical, *and* gendered Dasein. But the core motivation of Heidegger's early project is not to offer phenomenological investigations into the concreteness of bodily life. Rather, it is to inquire into the meaning of being of Dasein itself. And this inquiry ultimately leads us beyond the body and the hierarchical relations of sexual difference to the formal conditions of meaning. It is on the basis of these conditions that we can begin to make sense of things in the first place, and this making sense is itself made possible by the manifold "self-opening" of time.

Understanding the nature of Dasein's neutrality enables us now to broaden our discussion of the body-problem by focusing on Heidegger's analysis of Dasein's animal nature, and why, according to Heidegger, our own connectedness to animal life does not represent a condition for the possibility of meaning. This will help us understand what Heidegger means when he makes the controversial claim that only human practices are meaningful and animals are "world-poor" (*weltarm*) and, consequently, deprived of meaning.

Life, Logos, and the Poverty of Animals

Heidegger's 1929–30 Freiburg lecture course, "The Fundamental Concepts of Metaphysics," has been the focal point of much recent debate concerning the merits of his critique of metaphysical humanism, a critique that represents one of the core motivations of his early project. In this lecture course—devoted largely to theoretical biology—Heidegger appears to perpetuate the same oppositional prejudices of traditional humanism that he seeks to dismantle by arguing that there is a fundamental difference between animal "behavior" (*Benehmen*) and human "comportment" (*Verhalten*). This difference, according to Heidegger, leaves nature in the domain of "un-meaning" (*unsinniges*) and animals without an understanding of being because they are trapped in their environment by the "ring" (*Umring*) of their natural instincts and, as a result, remain "poor in world" (*weltarm*). This apparently negative portrayal of animal life persists throughout Heidegger's middle and later period. Indeed, one can find remarks on the poverty of animal life in any number of Freiburg lecture courses, including his 1934 lecture on Hölderlin's "*Germanien*" and "*Der Rhein*" poems, his 1942 Parmenides course, and his 1951–52 course "What Is Called Thinking?" In addition, the 1935 essay "The Origin of the Work of Art" and the famous "Letter on Humanism" of 1947 contain strong remarks that amplify the point that "animals are lodged in their respective environments [and] are never placed freely in the lighting of being, which alone is 'world' " (LH, 206).

Although criticisms of Heidegger's humanism and his dismissive treatment of animal life were initially introduced by his own students, Hans Jonas and Karl Löwith,[1] the question has been recently taken up by French interpreters such as Jacques Derrida, Didier Franck, Jean-Luc Nancy, and Michel Haar, as well Anglophone critics such as William McNeill, David Farrell Krell, Simon Glendinning, and Matthew Calarco.[2] While the critics acknowledge Heidegger's effort to dismantle the metaphysical legacy of Cartesian subjectivity—by interpreting the human being not as a self-contained subject that is set over and against objects but as Dasein, a historically situated *way of being* that is already "absorbed" (*aufgehen*) in a meaningful public world—there is no denying the inferior light cast on animal life. The argument suggests that Heidegger's substitution of the term *Dasein* for human being has done little to overcome the hierarchical distinction of man over animal. Indeed, Heidegger amplifies this point in his "Letter on Humanism" when he writes, "Traditional humanism is opposed because it does not set the *humanitas* of man high enough" (LH, 210).

What is largely missing in the critiques of Heidegger's alleged humanism, however, is an attempt to situate the discussion within the context of his overall project.[3] In this chapter, we will see that Heidegger's attempt to differentiate human from animal is to be understood only within the framework of a more fundamental question, the question of the meaning of being in general. In this regard, Heidegger's program is not overly concerned with humans (or animals) but with the temporal "event" (*Ereignis*) that "gives" (*gibt*) meaning to beings, enabling humans to talk about and make sense of animals in the first place. The "*humanitas* of man," in this regard, is not to be understood in terms of some metaphysical substance (soul, mind, reason) that separates human from animal. It is, rather, a reference to *logos* as an unfolding, linguistically structured space of meaning that is always already "there" (*Da*), already occurring in and through the social acts and practices of humans. It is only on the basis of *logos* that beings—including ourselves—can be understood. Indeed, based on Heidegger's view, the possibility of engaging the animal question from a standpoint that is logos-free, that is not already colored by "humanization," is absurd (N2, 99–105). Animals can reveal themselves *as* the kinds of beings that they are only by the space of meaning that arises through the shared practices of a historical people.

Dasein's Animal-Nature

Heidegger's analysis of Dasein's animal-nature stems from his critique of substance ontology, where traditionally the human being has been interpreted as a composite or unity of two substances, "mind/soul" and "matter/body" (BT, 74). This framework makes it possible to interpret the human being not only as living matter, a biological organism alongside other organisms, but as a thinking, conscious organism, a "rational animal."[4] Defining human existence in terms of being a special kind of living organism is, as we have repeatedly seen, an ontic, "zoological definition." On Heidegger's view, neither "*rationalitas* (rationality, consciousness, spirituality)" nor "*animalitas* (animality and corporeality)" captures the *essence* of being human (N3, 139–140; IM, 148).

Claiming that animals and humans are both living, biological beings insofar as they share objectively present characteristics—such as limbs, organs, reproductive systems, and physiological chemistry—will only tell us "what" these particular beings are. As we have seen, Heidegger's project is not concerned with the objective "whatness" of beings. He is concerned, rather, with the meaning of being itself, the unfolding movement of human life and how this movement is unique insofar as it discloses or lets beings come into being. The tradition, therefore, is unable to come to grips with, what Heidegger will call, the *humanitas* of the human being, the Da-sein understood as the disclosive "there" (*Da*), making it possible for entities to emerge-into-presence *as such*.[5]

In his 1929–30 lectures, Heidegger gives his most sustained argument for why humans are different from animals insofar as they embody an understanding of being and are, therefore, able to encounter beings *as such*. Animals do have something in common with humans, according to Heidegger, namely, access to beings—such as rocks, trees, and sun—but they do not encounter these things *as* "this, and not that," *as* rocks, trees, and sun. Animals, therefore, are "impoverished," or "world-poor" (*weltarm*), because they do not participate in the "to and fro," the shaping of and the being shaped by a world, by an intelligible background of sociohistorical relations (FCM, 211). Humans, on this view, are distinctive because they are "world-forming" (*weltbildend*). Thus,"the animal can have a world because it has access to entities," as Derrida explains, "but it is deprived of a world because it does not have access to entities *as such* in their being" (OS, 51).

Consequently, animals are "lodged in their respective environments," and for this reason their access to things is merely sensory or instinctual, based on seeing, smelling, and hearing, not of "understanding" (*Verstehen*), of encountering beings on the basis of a meaningful public world. Heidegger tries to make this point when he discusses the behavior of bees as an example of beings that are trapped within the "ring" (*Umring*) of instinctual drives that they are "subservient" to (FCT, 253–254). He describes an experiment—conducted by contemporary zoologist Jakob von Uexküll—with bees that continue to suck on a cup filled with honey even after their abdomens have been cut away, with the honey visibly streaming behind it.

> This shows convincingly that the bee by no means recog-
> nizes the presence of too much honey. It recognizes neither
> this nor even—though this would be expected to touch it
> more closely—the absence of its abdomen. . . . [The bee]
> continues its instinctual activity [*Treiben*] regardless, pre-
> cisely because it does not recognize that plenty of honey is
> still present. Rather, the bee is simply taken [*hingenommen*]
> by the food. . . . It is precisely being taken by its food that
> prevents the animal from taking up a position over and
> against the food. (FCM, 242)

Trapped in its instinctual ring, the bee does not recognize the honey
as such, as too much food. Driven by its instincts, it is held captive
by the food.[6] Although Heidegger recognizes that each species of animal has *"its own* specific ring," the ring does not allow the animal to
encounter things in terms of a referential context of meaning, a context
that allows beings to emerge as "this, not that" (FCM, 247). For this
reason, the way animals encounter beings is "fundamentally different
from the manifestness of beings as encountered in the world-forming
Dasein of man" (FCM, 277). Animal behavior is absolutely governed
by this circle of drives and is "closed off" to the world. Consequently,
animal "behavior" is fundamentally different from human activity
or "comportment."

> The specific manner in which man is we shall call *comport-
> ment* and the specific manner in which the animal is we
> shall call *behavior*. They are fundamentally different from
> one another. . . . The behavior of the animal is not a doing
> and acting, as in human comportment, but a driven per-
> forming. In saying this we mean to suggest that instinctual
> drivenness, as it were, characterizes *all* such animal perfor-
> mance. (FCM, 237)

For Heidegger, the word "comportment" is a broad reference to the
purposive, concrete practices of humans, practices that are always
directed toward a holistic totality of social relations. In the same way
that tools are related to one another in a workshop, these social relations cannot be understood in isolation; each event or thing can only
be understood in terms of the way it is directed toward other things
within a meaningful, referential background. Animals' behavior, on the
other hand, is defined not in terms of their relation to a meaningful
background but, rather, in terms of instinctual responses or "driven

performing" (*Treiben*), held "captive" by a ring of biological drives (FCM, 237). Behavior, therefore, is not meaningful, because only the world, the disclosive "there" (*Da*), "gives" meaning. For this reason, the animal *"behaves within an environment but never within a world"* (FCM, 239).

However, as many critics have pointed out, there are serious problems with Heidegger downplaying the role of our animal nature. Derrida, for instance, points out that Heidegger's analysis of animals largely overlooks the vast structural differences that separate one animal species from another. In the 1929–30 lecture course, Heidegger appears to interpret bees, worms, moles, and apes as all essentially the same, as organisms that are held captive by instinctual drives and have no access to beings *as such*. Derrida accuses Heidegger of assuming that animality "is one thing, one domain, one homogeneous type of entity, which is called animality *in general*, for which any example would do the job" (OS, 57). This homogeneous reading of animals not only fails to address the vast differences between lower forms of animal life and higher forms, it also neglects the possibility of a kinship between animals and humans in terms of social practices that may reveal a primitive type of world-forming in, for instance, higher mammals. Derrida amplifies this point in his second *Geschlecht* essay when he says this:

> Heidegger takes no account of a certain "zoological knowledge" that accumulates, is differentiated, and becomes more refined concerning what is brought together under this so general and confused word animality. (G2, 173)

Based on Heidegger's reading, animals are lumped together and closed off from the possibility of dwelling in the world.

Furthermore, Heidegger's sharp distinction between humans and animals is marked by language that is fundamentally hierarchical. If, as Heidegger says, animals are "impoverished," "poor," "captive," and "subservient," as he does in the 1929–30 lectures, then this vocabulary perpetuates the anthropocentric prejudices of traditional metaphysics by casting an inferior or a negative value on the domain of animals. As Derrida says:

> If privative poverty indeed marks the caesura or hand, between the animal and human Dasein . . . the fact remains that the very negativity, the residue of which can be read in this discourse on privation, cannot avoid a certain anthropocentric or even humanist teleology. (OS, 55)

Although his project seeks to overcome the detached, consciousness-centered assumptions of humanistic metaphysics, by excluding animals from world-forming Heidegger appears to perpetuate the same legacy embodied in Protagoras's dictum, one that now says, "[Dasein] is the measure of all things." On this view, it is only against the background of historically shaped, human-centered acts and practices that beings can be disclosed, emerging into presence from concealment. Heidegger's project remains, as Derrida says, a "reevaluation" or "revalorization of the dignity of man" (MP, 128).

Finally, Heidegger's account disregards the possibility of the animal's primitive but meaningful social language embodied in forms of gestures, cries, and expressions. In the *Phenomenon of Life*, Hans Jonas explains:

> Animals . . . have a mediated relationship with their environment due to their capacity for movement and the sensual perception of space and distance. With this sensual capacity animals are subjected to the possibility of suffering and, more importantly, begin to possess the rudiments of language. The animals can produce sounds that signal danger, the possibility of food, the approach of a mate, etc. . . . and such sounds are meaningful to it and other non-human organisms in their natural setting. Heidegger is oblivious to the primitive social expressions of animals. On Heidegger's account, it is not that animals possess an impoverished capacity of language, it is that they do not possess language at all, and this creates an unbridgeable gap between human beings and animals.[7]

Trapped in their instinctual drives, animals, according to Heidegger, are absolutely deprived of the possibility of speech, which would not only allow them to make sense of beings but would make it possible to confront the question of their *own* being. This results in the "abyss" between humans and animals, where "the leap from living animals to humans that speak is as large if not larger than that from the lifeless stone to living being."[8] For Heidegger, growing into language means growing into a prereflective familiarity with a sociohistorical background, and beings make sense *only on the basis of* this background. An animal, in response to Jonas's criticism, does indeed encounter beings and may communicate a threat or a need to mate, but only humans encounter beings in terms of how they meaningfully relate to other beings in a holistic nexus of social relations. Human life, on this account, is irrevocably welded to a world, an already understood space of meaning. To grasp this distinction, we must clarify the relationship between Heidegger's conceptions of "life" and "world," and in order to do this we must move away from the controversial 1929–30 lectures and go back a decade to Heidegger's first Freiburg period.

The Question of Life in the Aristotle Lectures

The question of "factical life" (*faktische Leben*) is explored in a number of places in Heidegger's early writings and lectures, notably his 1920 book review essay, "Comments on Karl Jaspers *Psychology of Worldviews*," his 1920–21 lectures, "The Phenomenology of Religious Life," and his 1923 summer course, "Ontology: The Hermeneutics of Facticity." However, it is Heidegger's 1921–22 winter semester lecture course, "Phenomenological Interpretations of Aristotle: Introduction to Phenomenological Research," that offers the most sustained and systematic treatment of the phenomenon of life. In these Aristotle lectures, Heidegger repeatedly acknowledges the deep influence that the "life-philosophy" (*Lebensphilosophie*) of Nietzsche, Bergson, Simmel, Scheler, and, most importantly, Dilthey had on his project, to the extent that they consistently emphasized the fundamental priority of factical life over the detached theorizing characteristic of traditional philosophy. From the perspective of *Lebensphilosophie*, the mainstream Cartesian account of the human being as a disembodied mind or subject that can impartially theorize about objects is derivative. Such a perspective is already shaped or mediated in advance by one's own "factical life," which is "being-there *for a while at a particular time*" (HF, 5, emphasis added).

Based on this view, life is not to be understood in terms of the self-regulating teleology of vitalism or the causally determined interactions of modern materialism. Life refers, rather, to the totality of sociohistorical relations that I am always already involved in, and it is this meaningful background that allows me to make sense of the entities that I encounter and handle every day. One's own lived situation, therefore, is to be understood in an "ultimate" sense, as a "primal phenomenon." It is the "starting point" of all philosophy. In *Pattern and Meaning in History*, Dilthey explains:

> Life, in this sense, extends over the whole range of objec-
> tive mind accessible to experience. Life is the fundamental
> fact which must form the starting point for philosophy. It

is that which is known from within, that behind which
we cannot go. Life cannot be brought before the judgment
seat of reason.[9]

Human life, therefore, cannot be reduced to the mechanistic functions of
the organism, functions that can be explained and quantified by modern
biology, because the traditional philosophic and scientific worldviews
are already colored by life, by an unfolding historical background of
assumptions, prejudices, customs, and institutions. Thus "One cannot dissect life into its constituent parts; it cannot be reduced to an
analysis," says Dilthey, "[indeed] thought cannot fully go behind life,
for it [thought] is the expression of life."[10] Indeed, we can only make
sense of biological entities on the basis of life understood in terms
of the concrete "movement" (*Bewegung*) of historical existence. In this
regard, any scientific/rational theorizing is itself a mode of philoso-
phi*zing*, a "living act" (*Vollzug*) that must be understood in terms of
"basic modes of life itself" (PIA, 62).[11] For this reason, according to
Heidegger, philosophy—at its most basic level—"cannot be defined
and ought not to be defined; philosophy can only be *'lived,'* and that
is the end of the story" (PIA, 13, emphasis added).

Heidegger, however, remained suspicious of *Lebensphilosophie* in
his early period, because the word "life" had never been clarified by
the philosophic tradition. It remained "ambiguous" (*vieldeutig*) and
"hazy" (*diesig*), loaded with competing interpretations (PIA, 62, 66).

> The term "life" is remarkably vague today. It is used to refer
> to a comprehensive, ultimate, and meaningful reality: "life
> itself." At the same time, the word is employed ambiguously:
> "political life," a "wretched life," "to bear a hard life," "to
> lose one's life on a sailing trip." (PIA, 62)

With Dilthey's project in mind, Heidegger saw "life-philosophy" inevitably succumbing to a form of "irrationalism," because it attempted
to create a foundation for "factical life" and the "human sciences"
(*Geisteswissenschaften*) by means of the same conceptually objective criteria as traditional epistemology and the "natural sciences"
(*Naturwissenschaften*). Such a project is impossible when one realizes
that any attempt to impartially isolate the objective structures of life
is already caught up in life. In short, theorizing about life is already
a mode of living. The result, for "life-philosophy," is the realization
that there can be no neutral, ahistorical standpoint, no "God's-eye

view" from which the structures of life become transparent. Dilthey recognized the tension.

> Between this reality of life and the scientific intellect there appears to be no possibility of comprehension, for the concept sunders what is unified in the flow of life. The concept represents something which is universally and eternally valid, independent of the mind which propounds it. But the flow of life is at all points unique; every wave in it arises and passes.[12]

Due to the internal contradictions of his own position, Dilthey ultimately abandoned his project, yielding to irrationalism in the form of historical relativism, concluding:

> The finitude of every historical appearance, be it religion or an ideal or a philosophical system, as well as the relativity of every kind of human comprehension of the totality of things, is the last word of the historical world-view, all flowing in a process, nothing enduring.[13]

Heidegger did not see *Lebensphilosophie* as necessarily irrational because it failed to fit into the epistemological categories of scientific and theoretical philosophy. For Heidegger, this simply shows that life philosophy uncritically adopted the objective measures of traditional philosophy rather than developing a systematic—and coherent—analysis of its own, one that allows the interpreter to gain a nonobjectifying access to the structures of life.[14] This analysis, initially introduced as the "hermeneutics of facticity," would become the famous "existential analytic" or "analytic of Dasein" in *Being and Time*. Relying on the "secret weapon" of his phenomenology—the methodological principle of "formal indication" (*formale Anzeige*)—Heidegger's project would begin by offering careful descriptions of phenomena as they initially show up or appear in concrete life.[15] However, because the movement of life resists conceptual representation, one's own *existentiell* descriptions are always merely "provisional" or "indicative" (*anzeigend*). They only "point to" a "way" or an "approach" to the ontological structures or "categories"—the "existentialia" in *Being and Time*—of life (PIA, 17).

Access to the structures of life, based on this view, is always "indeterminate" or impure, because the phenomenologist is already caught up in the concrete movement of his or her own life. For this

reason, there is nothing decisive or complete about the formal indication. It simply points, in a nonprejudicial way, to concrete possibilities
that can be factically lived out. In his 1920 course, "Phenomenology of
Intuition and Expression," Heidegger explains that the principle of formal indication is meant to always keep the phenomenologist in contact
with the dynamic movement of life. The result is a "non-prejudicing,
delimiting way of touching the factic by which, however, no decisive
results are produced."[16] This means that any "direction" or "approach"
to life "functions both to guide and to deter." Each approach reveals
one way to the structures of life but simultaneously conceals other
ways. As Heidegger says in his 1921–22 Aristotle lectures:

> The formal indication possesses, along with its referen-
> tial character, a prohibiting (deterring, preventing) one at
> the same time. As the basic sense of the methodological
> approach of phenomenological interpretation at all levels of
> actualization, the formal indication functions both (always
> "at the same time") to guide as well as to deter in various
> ways. (PIA, 105)

Thus the word "formal" in Heidegger's "formal indication" is misleading. The formal has nothing to do with traditional Platonic forms
understood as universal essences or general concepts. "The formal is
not the 'form,' and the indication its content," says Heidegger, "on
the contrary, 'formal' means 'approach toward the determination,'
approach-character" (PIA, 27). What is formally indicated by this
approach is the directionality of life, namely, that life—as ongoing
comportment, activity, or movement—is always "relational." In other
words, life has a prereflective intentional directedness, where we are
already "directing ourselves towards" or "being directed towards" a
meaningful nexus of equipment, practices, and others (BP, 58). Human
comportment, based on this view, is simply "a relation to something."[17]
Life in this regard must be understood in terms of a kind of instability or "restlessness" (*Unruhe*), insofar as it is always moving, always
directed toward particular concerns, needs, and wants.

    As we have already seen, when Heidegger employs the word
"world" (*Welt*) in his early lectures, he is not referring to a spatial
container filled with a collection of present-at-hand objects. Rather,
the world is the " 'wherein' a factical Dasein can be said to 'live' "
(BT, 93). It is the meaningful public background that I am concretely
involved with in the course of my daily life. Thus " 'world' immediately names—and this is crucial—*what* is lived, the content aimed at

in living, that which life holds to" (PIA, 65). The ongoing, relational nature of my "care" (*Sorge*) indicates what matters to me, what I am worried or concerned about. As a teacher in the "academic world," I am concerned *about* my students who are struggling in my class; my computer matters to me as a scholar because I use it *for* the composition of lectures and articles; I regularly hold office hours *for the sake of* my self-interpretation as a responsible teacher. Thus Heidegger says:

> Living, in its verbal meaning, is to be interpreted according to its relational sense as caring; to care *for* and *about* something; to live from [*on the basis of*] something, caring *for* it. (PIA, 68, emphases added)

To this end, life is always directed in advance toward a holistic background of social relations, what Heidegger simply calls the "towards-which." The totality of these social relations makes up, for example, the "academic world." And my involvement in the "academic world" is a *way of living*, one dimension of a wider context of ways of living in general. It represents the social expectations, needs, and practices that are part of a larger totality of social relations that Heidegger simply calls *"the* world" (BT, 119, emphasis added). This means the words "life" and "world" belong together.

> We could say that life is in itself world-related; "life" and "world" are not two separate self-subsistent Objects, such as a table and the chair which stands before it in a spatial relation. . . . The nexus of sense joining "life" and "world" is precisely expressed in the fact that, in characteristic contexts of expression in speech, the one word can stand in for the other: e.g., "to go out into life," "out into the world"; "to live totally in one's world," "totally in one's life." World is the basic category of the content sense in the phenomenon, life. (PIA, 65)

The movement of human life is distinct from that of animals, therefore, because it always points to a meaningful totality of public "references" and "assignments." In his 1923 lecture course "Ontology: Hermeneutics of Facticity," Heidegger offers an example of how we always encounter things in terms of this dense background of sociohistorical relations that allows things to count and matter in particular ways.

> What is there in the room there at home is the table (not
> "a" table among many other tables in other rooms and
> houses) at which one sits *in order to* write, have a meal,
> sew, play. Everyone sees this right away, e.g., during a visit:
> it is a writing table, a dining table, answering table—such
> is the primary way in which it is being encountered in
> itself.... Its standing-there in the room means: Playing this
> role in such and such characteristic use. This and that about
> it is "impractical," unsuitable. That part is damaged. It now
> stands in a better spot in the room than before—there's
> better lighting, for example. The boys like to busy them-
> selves at the table.... There that decision was made with
> a *friend* that time, there that *work* written that time, there
> that *holiday* celebrated that time. (HF, 69)

Based on this view, I am never simply bored, upset, or happy in
my everyday life, because these dispositions are always mediated in
advance by my relational involvement in a meaningful public world.
I am upset *about* my brother's divorce or the illness of a colleague
down the hall; I am happy *that* I was promoted at work or received
a financial windfall with the sale of some real estate.

    We can say, therefore, that it is because humans are invariably
engaged in a public space that is already saturated with social and
historical significance that they do not merely encounter things. Things
always affect humans in meaningful ways in terms of their relations
to other things and events, in terms of an "in-order-to" structure of
specific social purposes, goals, and functions.

> We can first fully understand what it "is" and means to live
> factically "in" meaningfulness. The abbreviated expression
> "to live in meaningfulness" means to live in, out of, and
> from objects whose content is of the [structural] character
> of the meaningful. (PIA, 70)

But life is more than the unfolding background that allows things to
meaningfully come into being *as such*. Caught up in the mundane
affairs and projects of everydayness, life also has a tendency to flee
from itself by trying to stabilize its own "movedness" (*Bewegtheit*).

    In exploring the various "categories of life" in the 1921–22 Aris-
totle lectures, Heidegger anticipates the moves that will become so
crucial in *Being and Time* by pointing out that our workaday activities
are—all too often—motivated by an inclination to "secure" or "dis-

tance" ourselves from the precariousness, instability, and "struggle" (*Kampf*) of life. By being "seduced" by the manifold affairs of the public world—shopping, working, traveling, gossiping, dining—the difficult questions of factical life are scattered and "dispersed" (*zerstreuen*). The public world "makes things easy" by giving life an illusory sense of security and stability (PIA, 81). Life, in this regard, ceaselessly flees from itself by being "hyperbolic" (*hyperbolisch*), rushing headlong into meaningful public projects, careers, and commodities that keep the instability that is always "before" us at bay. Heidegger explains:

> Factical life always seeks to make things easy; inclination goes along with the drift (*Zug*) of itself, without adding anything on, being-inclined corresponds to the pull, rushes towards it "without further ado." The "further ado" does not simply reside in the field of proclivity. Mundane difficulties are actually ways to take our ease. Along with convenience, life at the same time seeks the assurance that nothing can be closed off to it. . . . Living is caring and indeed is so in the inclination toward making things easy for oneself, in the inclination toward flight. (PIA, 81)

This means life is "guilty" (*Schuld*), because it is wrapped up in the assumptions, prejudices, and material things of the "present" (*Gegenwart*). As such, it covers over its own temporal and historical constitution, denying its genuine character of what Heidegger will call in *Being and Time* "thrown projection." Life, understood primordially, captures the sense of (1) being arbitrarily "thrown" (*geworfen*) into the "past" (*Gewesenheit*), an unfolding sociohistorical situation that determines the way things count and matter to us in terms of certain dispositions or moods (*Stimmung*) while (2) being "on the way" (*unterweg*), restlessly moving forward or "projecting" into future social goals and projects but always with the imminent possibility of death. By staying increasingly distracted by the immediate worries and concerns of the present, we remain severed from the temporal dimensions or "ecstasies" of past and future, from the original unsettledness of life as "thrown projection," an unsettledness that always comes "before" our daily comportment with a meaningful nexus of things. To this end, life has a tendency to "elude" itself, to not care about itself.

> In being transported by the meaningful things of the world, in the hyperbolic development of new possibilities of experiencing and caring for the world, factical life constantly

eludes itself as such. Insofar as it does so, explicitly or not, it is precisely present. The more life increases its worldly concern and the "before" is lost in the increased proclivity and expulsion of distance, all the more certainly does life then have to do with itself. In caring, life sequesters itself off from itself. (PIA, 80)

So not only is human life distinct insofar as it involves comportment, a relational, purposive doing and acting that allows things to emerge-into-presence *as such*, but it also carries the seeds of its own "ruinance" (*Ruinanz*); life lulls us to sleep by keeping us busily occupied with everyday worries and distractions, "sequestering" us from taking life seriously. "Ruinance," in this regard, must *not* be understood as something negative, something that can be avoided or overcome. Indeed, "ruinance" is a positive constitution of life's movedness, a "categorial structure of facticity" (PIA, 115). However, the structure of "ruinance" opens up an even deeper distinction—the possibility of human life to offer a "counter-ruinance" by announcing the precariousness and instability of its own movement, an announcement that is invariably accompanied by torment.

In outlining the temporal or "chairological" (*kairologisch*) characteristics of life in the 1921–22 Aristotle lectures, Heidegger claims that "ruinance" is akin to the "abolition of time," where life remains stuck in "what is," in the everyday fads and fashions of the present, and flees from its own "basic movedness" (PIA, 104). But life can also, "from time to time," announce the fact that it is *more* than the worldly affairs of the moment, *more* than the meaningful social norms and routines that give life a sense of stability and comfort. Heidegger refers to this as the "historiological" characteristic of life, a characteristic that demands a different disposition and can cause "something like torment (agony), affliction, and vexation" (PIA, 102). This other disposition involves a "questionability of life," one that owns up to the fact that we do not possess life as if it were a present-at-hand object—a linear sequence of minutes, hours, days, and weeks—to be manipulated and controlled. Rather, we are already possessed by life's fragile movedness, and we must be willing "to sit still, be able to wait, 'to give time' " (PIA, 103). Heidegger will refer to this authentic disposition as "a counter-ruinant movedness."

A counter-ruinant movedness is the one of the actualization of philosophical interpretation, and indeed it is actualized in the appropriation of the mode of access to questionability. It is precisely in questioning that factical life attains its genuinely developed self-givenness. (PIA, 113)

And maintaining this disposition is not easy. Heidegger makes it clear that it is a "constant struggle," a repeated "resistance" against the comforting busy-ness of the present (PIA, 114).

From this we can say that only humans are able to struggle, to open themselves up to, what Heidegger will call in *Being and Time*, life's "authentic possibilities," the fact that life unfolds as a disclosive horizon that allows beings to come into being, but it is a horizon that has a fundamentally unstable, abyssal structure insofar as it stretches backward toward an irretrievable past and forward toward possibilities that are "not yet" (BT, 222–223). For Heidegger, understanding this disclosive horizon in terms of its abyssal structure and how this horizon is closed off to animals can be properly grasped only by returning to the ancient Greek conception of meaning understood in terms of *logos*. The return to the question of logos will allow us to more carefully articulate what Heidegger means by the "poverty of animals."

Logos and the Animal Question

On Heidegger's view, the traditional interpretation of the human being as the *animal rationale* (*zōon logon echon*) is problematic, not just because it perpetuates the assumptions of substance ontology—interpreting the human being as *a* "rational living thing"—but because it misinterprets the Greek word *logos*. This misinterpretation stems from the Latinized translation of logos as "reason" or "rationality" (LS, 60). Early on in *Being and Time*, Heidegger suggests that "discourse" (*Rede*) is the proper rendering of logos. "The basic signification of logos," says Heidegger, "is 'discourse' . . . meaning to make manifest what one is 'talking about' in one's discourse" (BT, 56).

Rede is ordinarily translated as "discourse," "talk," or "speech," as in "*eine Rede halten*" ('to give a speech'), and it has long been understood as the essential faculty that distinguishes human beings from all other living things, making the human being human. In his 1950 lecture, "Language," Heidegger explains:

Man is said to have language by nature. It is held that man, in distinction from plant and animal, is the living being capable of speech. This statement does not mean only that, along with other faculties, man also possesses the faculty

of speech. It means to say that only speech enables man
to be the living being he is as man. (LA, 187)

However, in this passage, Heidegger is rejecting the traditional interpretation of *Rede* as an innate capacity for expression used to communicate information about objects. If this is the measure of language,
as commentators such as Hans Jonas and Michel Haar have pointed
out, then the chasm between human and animal is not so wide. The
audible cries and gestures of animals undoubtedly reveal a capacity
for designative expression.[18] For Heidegger, language is not a reference to lexical entities that signify various emotions, thoughts, and
states of affairs. Indeed, language is something that is not necessarily
linguistic at all.[19] Human expressions and gestures take place and
make sense only against a background of logos that is opened up by
the shared acts and practices of a historical people, a background that
allows me, for instance, to laugh at a political joke or feign indifference, smile sarcastically, lie to a colleague, or speak to my students
with an authoritative inflection but to my wife in a wholly different
tone. In short, it allows me to embody the particular practices of a
twenty-first-century American. Clifford Geertz explains this distinction
from the perspective of cultural anthropology.

> Our capacity to speak is surely innate; our capacity to speak
> English is surely cultural. Smiling at pleasing stimuli and
> frowning at unpleasing ones are surely in some degree
> genetically determined (even apes screw up their faces at
> noxious odors); but sardonic smiling and burlesque frowning
> are equally surely predominantly cultural, as is perhaps dem-
> onstrated by the Balinese madman who, like an American,
> smiles when there is nothing to laugh at. Between the basic
> ground places for our life that our genes lay down—the
> capacity to speak or to smile—and the precise behavior
> we execute—speaking English in a certain tone of voice,
> smiling enigmatically in a delicate social situation—lies a
> complex set of significant symbols under whose direction
> we transform the first into the second, the ground plans
> into the activity.[20]

Logos, in this regard, constitutes the meaningful "there" (*Da*), the
"referential context of significance" that we are involved in every day
(BT, 167). This means language is not to be understood zoologically,
as an innate capacity of the human being. Indeed, we *are* human

not because we speak but because we are "bespoken by" language. *"Language speaks.* It is language that first brings man about, brings him into existence" (LA, 190, 195).

Language, in this regard, brings beings into the open, into a public space of disclosure. And it is this aspect of dwelling in the open that animals are deprived of. In "The Origin of the Work of Art" (1935), Heidegger explains:

> [L]anguage is not only and not primarily an audible and written expression of what is to be communicated. . . . Language alone brings what is, *as* something that is, into the open for the first time. Where there is no language, as in the being of stone, plant, and animal, there is also no openness of beings. . . . Language, by naming beings for the first time, first brings beings to word and to appearance. (OWA, 185)

Logos, on this view, is what "makes manifest." It "lets something be seen" *as* the very thing that it is, constituting an open space of meaning or significance that always already shapes and determines the way we make sense of things. Thus "language," as Charles Guignon puts it, "is used not to refer to and communicate information about objects, but rather to open and articulate a public sense of meaningful concerns in which we find ourselves."[21]

In his 1935 Freiburg lecture course, "Introduction to Metaphysics," and later, in his 1944 course on Heraclitus, Heidegger will refer to logos as the *"hen panta,"* as that which "gathers everything" or "holds everything together" (IM, 142, 145). "[Logos] unifies by assembling. It assembles in that, in gathering, it lets lie before us what lies before *as such* and *as a whole*" (LS, 70, emphases added). Our workaday projects and relationships, our cultural institutions and religious habits, our monuments and holidays, and our artifacts and gestures are organized and held together by the public background or logos that allows beings to matter to us in particular ways. It is for this reason that Heidegger says "animals cannot speak." Animals have *phone*, voice, or sound and, therefore, have the capacity to signal a threat or a need to mate, but they do not dwell in logos.

It is because only human beings are appropriated by and belong to logos that Heidegger says animals are "world poor" (*weltarm*). Again, Heidegger is not concerned with "what" the animal "is" as an entity, whether this is understood in terms of the cause- and-effect functioning of mechanistic materialism or in terms of the self-causing, self-regulating teleology (or "entelechy") of vitalism. For Heidegger, the two prevailing views of life, "mechanism" and "vitalism," remain trapped within the tradition of substance ontology, attempting to give an account of the enduring "what-ness" of an entity. Such views fail to give an account of the animal's *way of being*, of "how" animals are. Heidegger realizes that the animal's way of being is one that is not, like the stone, absolutely deprived of world or "worldless" (*weltlos*), because the animal is "open" (*offen*) to an environment insofar as it has access to and can approach beings—water, trees, other animals (FCM, 198). However, as we saw earlier, this access to beings is reduced to what Heidegger calls "captivation" (*Benommenheit*), where the animal is trapped within a "ring" (*Umring*) of instinctual drives (FCM, 253).

This raises the question of *when*, in our own development, human beings actually become Dasein. One could argue that Heidegger's account of animals—as beings captivated by a ring of instincts—can also be applied to humans at the level of prelinguistic infant. The newborn child, like the animal, has access to beings and has the sentient capacity to feel—happy, afraid, excited—but is unable to articulate what she or he is fearful *for* or excited *about* and for this reason cannot be understood as a being that "exists," insofar as existence captures the sense of being meaningfully engaged in the world. The child, in this sense, is "poor in world" (*weltarm*), because she or he has not begun to master the relational background of social acts and practices that constitutes the world. The child is not yet opening the refrigerator "in-order-to" eat a snack or turning on the television "for-the-sake-of" being entertained. The ability to articulate the relational "for-the-sake-of-which" (*Worumwillen*), that is, to identify what one is concerned *for* or *about*, is one of the distinguishing characteristics of the being of Dasein.

However, to the extent that the child is immediately immersed in a meaningful public background, she or he quickly grows into Dasein, embodying the intelligible skills, roles, and norms characteristic of being-in a particular world. Hubert Dreyfus offers an example of this by drawing on a comparison of the child-rearing practices in Japan with those in the United States.

> A Japanese baby seems passive. . . . He lies quietly . . . while his mother, in her care, does [a great deal of] lulling, carrying, and rocking of her baby. She seems to try to soothe and quiet the child, and to communicate with him physically rather than verbally. On the other hand, the American infant is more active . . . and exploring of his environment,

and his mother, in her care, does more looking at and chatting to her baby. She seems to stimulate the baby to activity and vocal response. It is as if the American mother wanted to have a vocal, active baby, and the Japanese mother wanted to have a quiet, contented baby. In terms of styles of caretaking of the mothers in the two cultures, they get what they apparently want. . . . A great deal of cultural learning has taken place by three to four months of age . . . babies have learned by this time to be Japanese and American babies.[22]

What is suggested here is that before the child learns to talk—or even walk for that matter—she or he is already learning how to be a "self" (*Selbst*) by being immersed in logos as the common background of social acts, expressions, gestures, and customs that shapes the child's sense of who she or he is, allowing the child to understand and make sense of things, including herself or himself. The child, therefore, moves quickly from being "poor in world" to a being that is "world-form-ing" (*weltbildend*). The animal, because it is trapped within its own instinctual drives, is incapable of this kind of meaningful acculturation, and is, therefore, deprived of the possibility of "selfhood" (*Selbstheit*) (FCM, 238–239).

We can now better understand logos as the medium that arises out of the shared acts and practices of a historical people, and it is a medium that human beings immediately grow into and one that colors all of their factical experiences. "[We] everywhere and continually stand within it," says Heidegger, "wherever and whenever we comport ourselves with beings" (N4, 153). In *Being and Time*, he writes:

This everyday way in which things have been interpreted [in language] is one into which Dasein has grown in the first instance, with never a possibility of extrication. In it, out of it, and against it, all genuine understanding, interpreting, and communicating, all rediscovering and appropriating anew, are performed. In no case is a Dasein untouched and unseduced by this way in which things have been inter-preted, set before the open country of a "world-in-itself" so that it just beholds what it encounters. (BT, 213)

Acculturated into logos, humans are already tuned to the public world, to a shared social context that shapes their individual moods, dispositions, and temperaments. Logos, in this regard, is "like a [public] *atmosphere* in which we first immerse ourselves in each case and which then attunes us through and through" (FCM, 67). Indeed, it is only on the basis of logos that we can be in a mood in the first place. As we saw in chapter 1, "moods" (*Stimmung*) are not self-contained or encapsulated inside me. I am in a mood only by being *ek-static*, of "standing outside" of myself by my situated involvement in the world. This involvement determines in advance the way things affect me. Moods, on this account, are not a by-product of my animal physiology, of chemical imbalances or genetic predispositions. Heidegger would not deny these physiological aspects of our bodily being, for instance, the shortness of breath or racing heart that might accompany the mood of fear. But this is an observation based on what Heidegger calls the "ontic" aspect of moods, pertaining only to the objective "what-ness" of human beings.

For Heidegger, it is only the basis of a more fundamental "ontological problem," namely, our historical existence, our engagement in a public world or "there" (*Da*), that moods can arise (BT, 234). In other words, things matter to me *not* because my heart is racing or because I cannot catch my breath. I embody a certain temperament—a fear *about* my upcoming lecture at a conference, for instance—because my life is always shaped in advance by a particular historical situation, one where, in my case, impressing colleagues and giving public lectures matters to me as a college professor. Moods, therefore, are possible only on the basis of a public world.

> The dominance of the public way in which things have been interpreted has already been decisive even for the possibilities of having a mood—that is, for the basic way in which Dasein lets the world "matter" to it. The "they" [*das Man*] prescribes one's state-of-mind. (BT, 213)

Logos, in this regard, articulates the unfolding historical space of meaning, making it possible for us to be attuned to things. The animal is not tuned in this way because it is held captive by instinctual responses. The animal may be indifferent or angry, but it cannot meaningfully articulate what it is indifferent *toward* or angry *about*. The animal's way of being, as William McNeill writes, is "ahistorical. . . . [It] is excluded from an active participation in the temporality of the world as such."[23] This goes for all perceptual/sensual capacities—for seeing, hearing, touching, tasting—that humans share with animals.

In his 1929–30 lectures, and again in his 1944 lectures on Heraclitus, Heidegger makes this point explicit. In the case of hearing, for example, Heidegger claims that the "anatomically and physiologically identifiable ears, as the tools of sensation, never bring about a hearing, not even if we take this solely as an apprehending of noises, sounds, and tones" (LS, 65). Human beings do not hear things because they, like other animals, are anatomically equipped with ears. Bare sounds or noises may activate the body's audio equipment, but this is not hearing. Hearing occurs because these sounds are already colored by the world, already "fraught with meaning" (TDP, 60). It is only then that we have a perception *of* something, "the thunder *of* the heavens, the rustling *of* the woods, the gurgling *of* the fountains, the ringing *of* plucked strings, the rumbling *of* motors, [and] the noises *of* the city" (LS, 65, emphases added). Bodily perceptions make sense to us because we already dwell in meaning.

The same can be said for other body parts that animals apparently share with humans. In his 1951–52 lecture, "What Is Called Thinking?," Heidegger remarks that, although they have organs that can grasp things, "[animals] do not have hands."

> The hand is part of the bodily organism. But the hand's essence can never be determined, or explained, by its being an organ which can grasp. Apes, too, have organs that can grasp, but they do not have hands. The hand is infinitely different from all the grasping organs—paws, claws, or fangs—different by an abyss of essence. Only a being who can speak, that is, think, can have hands and can handily achieve works of handicraft. (WCT, 16)

The animal can certainly take hold of and manipulate things, but it does not use "handy" (*zuhanden*) equipment, because it does not encounter things in terms of a whole referential context or "totality of equipment" (*Zeugganze*). In my everyday practices, I already embody a prereflective understanding of a worldly context that allows a piece of equipment to show up *as such*. For instance, my university computer is not understood in isolation; it makes sense to me *as* a computer only insofar as I already embody a tacit familiarity with a whole nexus of cultural equipment and practices—the printer, the desk, the lamp, the chair, students, and colleagues—that constitutes what it means *to be* a professor in the modern academic world. In short, it is only on the basis of being absorbed into language (*logos*)—into a whole sociocultural context that already guides my roles, values, and practices—that beings are disclosed *as such*, enabling me to handle things in meaningful ways. When I wave to a friend, open the door, pick up the coffee cup, and put on my wristwatch, I am revealing how I am already shaped by and understand the world. Thus "the hand's gestures," says Heidegger, "run everywhere through language" (WCT, 16). Because the animal is not appropriated by the "event" (*Ereignis*) that gives meaning, it is deprived of dwelling in a world, "in truth."

However, the claim that humans dwell in meaning becomes problematic, particularly in *Being and Time*, when Heidegger claims that "[Dasein] is in the truth *and in untruth* equiprimordially" (BT, 272, emphasis added). According to Heidegger, when we are caught up in our everyday acts and practices, we dwell "in untruth," because we have a tendency to "fall" (*verfallen*) into the workaday roles and routines of the public world. We simply follow what anyone and everyone (*das Man*) is doing at the moment as we go about our daily lives. As David Krell reminds us, Heidegger's account of living "in untruth" in *Being and Time* is strikingly similar to the account of animal life in the 1929–30 lectures. In this inauthentic state, we are, like the bee buzzing toward the flower, completely "captivated," "dazed," and "benumbed" (*benommen*) by the circle of familiar routines and curiosities, concerned only with immediate goals and projects.[24] In "Introduction to Metaphysics," Heidegger will go so far as to suggest that when we are "absorbed" (*aufgehen*) in the public world in this way, we live like animals.

> [We] just reel about within the orbit of [our] caprice and lack of understanding. [We] accept as valid only what comes directly into [our] path, what flatters [us] and is familiar to [us]. *[We] are like dogs.* (IM, 141, emphases added)

Entangled in the needs and concerns of the present, we mechanically drift through our days, never looking too far forward into the future or too far backward into the past. Consequently, we lose sight of a more primordial sense of our own temporal constitution. We forget that we are finite beings who have been arbitrarily "thrown" into an unfolding historical situation, as we ceaselessly "project" forward into social possibilities, possibilities that culminate in death.

Yet to say that we invariably fall prey to the latest social fads and fashions is not to say that inauthentic Dasein is—like an animal—"poor in world." To be inauthentic is to dwell in meaning, to be caught up in a public understanding of a familiar, meaningful world. It is "in untruth," however, precisely because it is a way of being that creates an illusion of security and permanence about our existence and is forgetful of the fundamental contingency and unsettledness that underlies it.

This uniquely human kind of forgetfulness also results in a uniquely human kind of suffering, "anxiety" (*Angst*). As we have already seen, the significance of a mood such as anxiety is not determined by our animal physiology. Humans can be anxious only because they belong to the world in a particular way, a way that makes the physiological experience of anxiety possible. "Only because Dasein is anxious in the very depths of its being," says Heidegger, "does it become possible for anxiety to be elicited physiologically" (BT, 234).

Anxiety is a mood that discloses *my own* potentiality for death by revealing the precariousness and instability of the world as the original source of meaning, a source that—in the course of my quotidian affairs—grounds my being, giving purpose and direction to my life.[25] Anxiety, in this regard, is not to be confused with fear of this or that thing. One is anxious in the face of no-thing, in the face of the abyssal nature of the world *as a whole*. The temporal "event" (*Ereignis*) that grounds the world, making the disclosiveness of the "there" (*Da*) possible, is not anything permanent; it is nothing and nowhere. In anxiety, we experience the nothing as the collapse of meaning, where beings no longer make sense, emerging as meaningless in their bare "is-ness" (BT, 321). This experience opens up the possibility for a deeper, more authentic understanding of the entire "abyss [*Abgrund*]" of Dasein, the contingency and emptiness that grounds the world and myself (BT, 194). In these moments, I realize that I have no power over this ground, that the meaningful social possibilities opened up by logos are not my own, that I am not the basis for my own being. Heidegger writes, " 'Being-a-basis' means never to have power over one's ownmost being from the ground up. This 'not' belongs to the existential meaning of 'thrownness.' It itself, being a basis, *is* a nullity of itself" (BT, 330). Anxiety, in this regard, calls me to face the death that "*is in each case mine*" (BT, 67). Here death is to be understood not as biological "perishing" or "demise" (*Ableben*) but as the structure of nothingness that always underlies *my* time.[26]

By pulling us out of our tranquilizing routines, anxiety makes it possible for us to soberly acknowledge our own vulnerability, that there is nothing fixed and constant about existence, that to be Dasein is to be determined by a "*not*" (BT, 330). Based on Heidegger's view, because we alone have been appropriated by the abyssal "event" (*Ereignis*), we alone can be held out into the nothing, capable of experiencing death *as* death, as the merciless withdrawal of meaning. *Ereignis*, in this regard, is the abyssal ground that makes meaning possible, yet it simultaneously threatens to obliterate meaning. " 'Ground' [is] only accessible as meaning," says Heidegger, "even if that meaning itself is an abyss of meaninglessness" (BT, 194). Only humans can experience their own death, their own groundlessness, in this way. Animals, as beings trapped in biological instincts, do not confront the abyss; they merely "perish"; they "cannot die."[27]

The Animal Lectures in Context

Understanding Heidegger's lifelong project as one that is ultimately concerned with the "event" (*Ereignis*) that reveals and conceals beings allows us to see the hierarchical distinction between human and animal in its proper context. Although Heidegger insists that humans are distinct from animals because they are, among other things, engaged in a social world, dwell in language, embody the capacity to handle tools, and experience anxiety in the face of death, the goal was to "press on" beyond the concrete descriptions of human ways of being to get at the "worldly character of the world," namely, the conditions of meaning for intraworldly beings (FCM, 177–178). Thus the discussions of bodily organs, biology, and animal behavior in the 1929–30 lectures must be understood in terms of Heidegger's fundamental task. The entire analysis regarding the distinctions between the "world-less" (*weltlos*) stone, the "world-poor" (*weltarm*) animal, and the "world-forming" (*weltbildend*) human is important only insofar as it gives us access to the question of the meaning of being (FCM, 177–178). The extensive engagement with zoology in these lectures merely provides a path that points out the essential structures that constitute the world understood as the *ek-static* place that "gives" (*gibt*) meaning to beings.

Many commentators suggest that the "turn" (*Kehre*) away from the analysis of human existence—an analysis still very much a part of the 1929–30 lectures—to an account of the "event" (*Ereignis*) that gives meaning is characteristic only of Heidegger's later writings, beginning specifically with his *Contributions to Philosophy*, written during the period 1936–1938. Yet the theme of *Ereignis* persists throughout Heidegger's career and can already be found in his earliest writings and lectures.[28] The primary evidence for this is in his course during the 1919 War Emergency Semester entitled "Towards the Definition of Philosophy." It is in these first Freiburg lectures that the core breakthrough of Heidegger's entire project is introduced, namely, unearthing the primal, impersonal event that gives meaning.

In these lectures, Heidegger attempts to give an account of how everyday human experience is already saturated with significance. Speaking to his students in the lecture hall, Heidegger explains how, when walking into the room, he initially "sees the lectern." In seeing it, he does not theoretically construct brown surfaces onto rectangular shapes and construe what is seen as a lectern. Rather, the lectern is experienced immediately *as such*, as something familiar and significant. "The lectern is given immediately in the lived experience of it. I see it *as such*" (TDP, 71, emphasis added). It is not brown, box-shaped sense data. Rather, it is the teacher's lectern. It is the place where he sets his books and pens. It is in the room where he teaches philosophy, and outside the room lie the campus, other buildings, sidewalks, and trees. In short, he "sees the lectern in [terms of] an orientation, an illumination, *a background*" (TDP, 60, emphasis added). The lectern makes sense to Heidegger due to its place in a coherent unity of experiences and things, a referential context of relations that make up the totality of the academic world. And his involvement in the academic world is one way of living, one dimension of a wider context of ways of living in general. Academic life, in this regard, is itself part of a larger totality of meaningful social relations and practices.

Heidegger will refer to this pretheoretical totality as the "primal source" (*Ur-sprung*) of meaning into which we are totally "absorbed" (*aufgehen*) in the course of our everyday practices. For Heidegger, the factical human being—understood in these early lectures as the "historical I" and later as Dasein—is completely "given over" (*hingegeben*) to this primal something (TDP, 74–75). We belong to it and are appropriated by it. "In seeing the lectern," says Heidegger, "I am fully present in my 'I'; it resonates with the experience, as we said, it is an experience proper (*eigens*) to me and so do I see it. However, it is not a process but rather an *event of appropriation (Ereignis)*" (TDP, 63).[29] The lived-experience of the lectern, therefore, is not of an object that I am theoretically conscious of. The lectern immediately emerges as something meaningful because my life is already woven into "It" (*Es*), into this historical "event" (*Ereignis*). Indeed, it is only on the basis of being appropriated by the event that the traditional philosophic distinctions of "inner" (psychical) and "outer" (physical) can manifest in the first place. Heidegger explains:

> [The] event of appropriation is not to be taken as if I appropriate the lived experience to myself from outside or from anywhere else; "outer" and "inner" have as little meaning here as "physical" and "psychical." (TDP, 64)

The lectern already reveals itself *as* a lectern before I can begin to reflect on its objective properties, as something that is rectangular, brown, and box-shaped. For Heidegger, this means I already live in meaning, "in truth," before I can even make propositional truth claims. In other words, before I can judge whether or not the proposition, "The lectern is in the classroom," is true or false, things such as lecterns and classrooms have to already make sense to me. I must already be appropriated by and live through the event that allows the lectern to reveal itself, to emerge immediately as something familiar and significant for me. Only then can I make judgments about its objective status.

Here we have the initial formulation of the famous "ontological difference" between beings and being (understood in this case as meaning).[30] To this end, the young Heidegger is deeply influenced by a conception of logic developed by neo-Kantian philosopher Emil Lask (1875–1915).[31] For Lask, the positive sciences and traditional formal logic are concerned with things, namely, "what is"—matter, numbers, predicates, and propositions. Lask's version of transcendental logic, however, is not concerned with "what is" but with "what holds" things in truth, in meaning.[32] According to Lask, in our everyday experiences, things are already categorized as meaningful because they are shaped in advance by a logical space or framework of "non-entitative" categories or conditions—what Heidegger will refer to in *Being and Time* as "existentialia"—that endows things with meaning. Lask refers to this logical space as a "panarchy of the logos," the pre-objective domain of meaning *on the basis of which* things are rendered significant, intelligible, and "in the truth."[33] To say beings are "in the truth" is to say they make sense or are intelligible because they are already held together and categorized by the referential structures of logos, structures that open up a disclosive "there" (*Da*). It is for this reason that Heidegger says, "Lask discovered *the* world" (TDP, 104).

Interpreting logos in terms of the "primal source" that gives meaning allows Heidegger to intercept the criticism that his 1929–30 lectures perpetuate the kind of hierarchical and anthropocentric prejudices that have long characterized the Western tradition. Heidegger's project is not primarily concerned with human practices. His core concern is with the primal origin or source of meaning itself, with "the 'there' (*das 'Da'*), that is, the lighting of being" that makes human practices meaningful in the first place (LH, 205). As we saw in chapter 3, the lighting of being is not hierarchical or prejudiced but "neutral." It is prior to any bifurcated historical or cultural worldview that distinguishes man from woman or human from animal. Indeed, humans can make judgments about animals and others only *on the basis of* a neutral space of meaning.

As the primal source of any meaningful experience whatsoever, Dasein makes it possible to have a particular worldview, allowing beings to reveal themselves in different ways for different peoples. In his 1919 lectures, Heidegger points out how the modern European—understood as the subject that masters and controls nonhuman objects—makes sense of things only in terms of a particular historical world; the "farmer from deep in the Black Forest" dwells in another world; the "[tribesman] from Senegal" in another (TDP, 60). This means that the prevailing anthropocentric worldview of man over animal is simply one manifestation of Dasein. The space of meaning may be different for indigenous Americans, Japanese, and Inuit. For instance, Chief Seattle's reply to the U.S. government in 1852 concerning the purchase of tribal lands provides an example of a nonhierarchical manifestation of logos.

> The President in Washington sends word that he wishes to buy our land. . . . The idea is strange to us. . . . We know the sap which courses through the trees as we know the blood that courses through our veins. We are part of the earth and it is part of us. The perfumed flowers are our sisters. The bear, the deer, the great eagle, these are our brothers. The rocky crests, the juices in the meadow, the body heat of the pony, and man, all belong to the same family. . . . The shining water that moves in the streams and rivers is not just water, but the blood of our ancestors. If we sell our land, you must remember that it is sacred.[34]

Although historical peoples differ in terms of how they make sense of intraworldly beings, we are all already shaped by logos as the neutral source of meaning, a source that is prior to the understanding of any particular human being. Heidegger explains:

> For it is not the case that the human being first exists and then also one day decides amongst other things to form a world. Rather, world-formation is something that occurs, and only on this ground can a human being exist in the first place. (FCM, 285)

Because "It worlds" (Es weltet), humans are always "there" (Da) in meaning, continually shaping and being shaped by logos (TDP, 61). Logos does not occur independently of humans but in and through humans, who are already dispersed and absorbed in it. "World-formation," as William McNeill puts it, "is not something that the human being accomplishes in and through his or her actions; rather, it first enables our very being, our self-understanding and ability to relate to ourselves as beings that are already manifest."[35] This is why Heidegger went to such great lengths to avoid the traditional designation of human being as a "subject" or "substance." "We avoid these terms [subject, soul, consciousness, spirit, person]—or such expressions as 'life' and 'man'—in designating those entities that we are ourselves" (BT, 72). From the very beginning, Heidegger's core concern was with Dasein as "being-*the*-there" (not the "being there" of an individual in a determinate place and time), with the worldly openness that "gives" (*gibt*) meaning, allowing beings to emerge-into-presence *as such*.[36]

Now that we have situated the various criticisms concerning the neglect of the body within the context of Heidegger's overall project, we can draw a number of conclusions. First, Heidegger's conception of Dasein is, first and foremost, not to be interpreted in terms of an embodied agent with feelings, perceptions, and emotions. It signifies, rather, an unfolding background or space of meaning that is already there, prior to any embodied experience or capacity. Second, the "there"—the *Da* of Dasein—makes it possible for me to make sense of my feelings, perceptions, activities, and emotions. It is only because I dwell in a space of meaning that I can come to understand my embodied acts and practices for what they are. Third, the body certainly gives us access to beings, but it does not constitute a disclosive horizon that gives meaning to beings. Indeed, my body—like all beings—makes sense to me only on the basis of an already opened horizon. It is for this reason that I never encounter naked sense data in my everyday life. I encounter things that are already colored with historical and cultural significance, already "fraught with meaning" (TDP, 60).

Prelude to a Theory of Embodiment

As we move toward the concluding chapters, I want to suggest that simply because the body plays a derivative, ontic role in Heidegger's program does not mean that Heidegger fails to make a significant contribution to theories of embodiment. As we have seen, Heidegger acknowledges that the human body belongs to both earth and world. As material, earthly beings, we inhabit a specific sex, have a unique neurological, hormonal, and skeletal signature, and are capable of certain kinds of physiological movements, gestures, and sounds. As worldly beings, our corporeal attributes are made meaningful through our engagement in a shared, sociohistorical situation. In this regard, our bodily gestures, movements, and expressions always belong to a cultural background of lived acts and practices.[37] Traces of our world and history are inscribed in the body in our posture and gait, in the various aches and pains we carry, and in the anxieties that overwhelm us. The body, in this regard, is more than an encapsulated, dermal wrapping that houses organs, bones, and blood. The body is always *ek-static*, surpassing the limits of its own skin insofar as it is already shaping and being shaped by the world.

In the final chapters, this insight will be explored in light of Heidegger's later writings on modern technology. In these writings, Heidegger offers a groundbreaking analysis of life in an accelerated, overstimulated age, where the more we try to quantify, master, and control beings—including our own bodies—the more we are closed off from the ontological openness that offers other possibilities for Dasein. The consequences of the modern worldview are twofold. First, our everyday understanding becomes more contracted and narrow as beings show up exclusively as resources to be managed, consumed, and produced. Second, this harried, instrumental way of being fails to prepare us for the fundamental moods of anxiety and boredom that remind us of the frailty and finitude of the human condition. As a response to this worldview, we will explore the role that leisurely and festive dwelling plays in Heidegger's thought as a noninstrumental way of being that has the potential to free us from the cycles of technological busy-ness and to give us an opening to face and preserve the awesome abyss that underlies our own being.

Before moving on, it is important to note that I will be referencing Heidegger's later writings, beginning with *Contributions to Philosophy* (1936–38), yet these references will remain within the horizon of Heidegger's earlier analysis of everyday being-in-the-world. Much has been made regarding the "turn" (*Kehre*) in Heidegger's thought in the mid-1930s away from the project of *Being and Time*. This project, as we have seen, begins with the existential analysis of ontic Dasein in order to gain access to the ontological structures that, taken together, constitute the temporal "event" (*Ereignis*) or "clearing" (*Lichtung*) that makes any understanding of beings possible. This transcendental approach, as Heidegger makes clear in the "Letter on Humanism," fails to overcome the Western metaphysical tradition, because it is still trapped in the "language of metaphysics," employing objectifying, neo-Kantian concepts such as "transcendence," "horizon," and "condition of possibility" (LH, 231).[38]

Although Heidegger clearly distinguishes being (understood as the emergence of meaning) from beings (understood as entities), the goal of the early project is still to identify the metaphysical ground that gives meaning to beings.[39] The result is a tendency to represent what is ontological—namely, the meaning of being—in terms of an object, reifying the happening or event of being as *a* being, as something ontic, that is, *a* "horizon," *a* "clearing," or *a* "there." The language of *Being and Time*, in this regard, is unable to think the historical/temporal unfolding of being as such, what Heidegger will later call "be-ing-historical thinking" (*seynsgeschichtliches Denken*), because it is still too indebted to a representational tradition that objectifies being. In his *Contributions to Philosophy*, Heidegger describes this earlier failure in the following way:

> [In *Being and Time*] [w]e grasp the "ontological"—even as condition for the "ontic"—still only as an addendum to the ontic. . . . By this approach be-ing itself is apparently still made into an object, and the most decisive opposite of that is attained which the course of the question of be-ing has already opened up itself. (CP, 317)

After the turn, Heidegger's goal is to think the historical occurrence of be-ing as such, without the representational analysis of (human) beings, which means "the representation of 'transcendence' in *every* sense must *disappear*" (CP, 152). This shift requires a "leap," or letting go, of all objectifying language and occurs not by a subjective act of free will but out of a necessity made possible by the historical movement of be-ing itself.[40]

Acknowledging the significance of the turn, it is important for the reader to know that my attempt to appropriate a theory of embodiment from Heidegger in the concluding chapters should be read primarily as a supplement to the existential analytic of Dasein. Thus even though I will be referring to writings after the turn, these references are used only to fortify Heidegger's account of everyday being-in-the-world. This will also result in a change in the tone of the book, away from the close, textual analysis of Heidegger's writings and lectures to a broader, interdisciplinary reading that brings the question of embodied agency in Heidegger into conversation with critical social theory, medicine, and psychotherapy. The goal here is to see that even though the question of Dasein's bodily nature is ontic and preparatory, derivative of a deeper, ontological question—namely, the question of the meaning of being in general—Heidegger's account of existence in the age of global technology provides a fruitful opening through which we can explore how the body is formed and deformed by its engagement in and with the world.

The Accelerated Body

In 1881, physician George M. Beard introduced the phrase "neuras-thenia" to capture the emotional flatness and exhaustion from a life increasingly mediated by the mechanized acceleration and time pres-sure of the industrial age. According to Beard, it is not civilization that causes this kind of emotional strain but the unique social forms of modernity itself. "The Greeks were certainly civilized," says Beard, "but they were not nervous, and in the Greek language there is no word for the term."[1] By the late nineteenth century, neurasthenia had become a ubiquitous symptom of an overstimulated urban existence. Indeed, it can be argued that emotional exhaustion and bodily stress—emerging in the wake of the technological advent of speed and the compression of time and space—is *the* most distinctive characteristic of modern living and may represent what historian Arnold Toynbee calls "the most difficult and dangerous of all the current problems [that we face today]."[2]

Exposing the downside of technological acceleration is an enduring theme in Heidegger's thought. As early as his 1921–22 Freiburg lecture course on Aristotle, Heidegger was questioning the "untrammeled, explosive rushing" of everyday existence, identifying "unrest" (*die Unruhe*) as one of the central characteristics of inauthen-ticity, referred to in these early lectures as "ruinance" (*die Ruinanz*) (PIA, 111). A ruinant life, for Heidegger, is the life of "anyone" and "everyone" (*das Man*), a life where one "has no time" because one is endlessly consuming and managing "what is"—gadgets, informa-tion, resources, others (PIA, 104). Heidegger expands on this theme of the velocity of modern life in his *Contributions to Philosophy* when he identifies "acceleration" (*Beschleunigung*)—understood as the aspect of life shaped by "the mechanical increase of technical 'speeds' " and the "mania for what is surprising, for what immediately sweeps [us] away and impresses [us]"—as one of the fundamental "symptoms" of the technological age, along with "calculation" and the "outbreak of massiveness" (CP, 84). We can turn to an examination of these three overlapping symptoms in order to see how they form and de-form the body.

Technological Existence

Written during the period 1936–1938, Heidegger's *Contributions to Philosophy* is considered his most important book after *Being and Time* (1927). The book consists of six "joinings" or "fugues" (*Fügungen*) that—taken together—repeat the same disclosive movement of Western history from different perspectives.[3] The first fugue, "Echo," is the primary focus of this chapter. Echo signals the end of metaphysics, intimating the total withdrawal of the "question of being" in the age of global technology. As we saw in chapter 1, the distinctively Western understanding of being is moving toward its nihilistic end point in the technological age. "Nihilism" occurs when we no longer ask the ontological question concerning the being of beings—of *how* and *why* beings manifest or show up *as* they do—and are instead totally occupied with consuming, exchanging, and producing beings. In the age of nihilism, the world is understood solely as an object-region to be manipulated and quantified by "machination" (*Machenschaft*). With global machination, beings *are* only to the extent that they are "re-presentable," "made," or "can be made" in terms of calculable production and exchange (CP, 88–93).

What is significant in *Contributions* is the way in which our contemporary forgetfulness of the question of being is felt. Heidegger refers to this feeling as "horror" or "shock" (*Schreck*), a shock accompanied by "compelling distress" (*nötigende Not*) (CP, 79). However, what is particularly shocking today *"is the lack of distress"* itself; our way of living is so harried, busy and occupied with things that we have no time for distress (CP, 79, 277). In order to come to grips with the ways in which modern life embodies a hidden distress, we must revisit what Heidegger means by the self.

Again, for Heidegger, the human being (*Dasein*) is not to be interpreted in terms of a quantifiable material body. Dasein is a shared, sociohistorical "happening" (*Geschehen*) or *way of being* that opens up a horizon of intelligibility, a horizon that shapes the way beings are understood and matter to us in our everyday lives. The self, based on this view, is always already "absorbed" (*aufgehen*) in a public horizon and is properly understood not in terms of its objective properties but in terms of what it does every day and for the most part. This means

I am invariably involved in the activities that "They" or "Anyone" (*das Man*) are involved in; I have been "dispersed" (*zerstreuen*) into the public roles and practices of others.

Shaped by a public world, we invariably "fall prey" (*verfallen*) to modern assumptions, prejudices, and social fads. In today's turbo-capitalist economy, for instance, the self is interpreted as an autonomous subject who, for the most part, values busy-ness, careerism, and conspicuous consumption. Such public self-interpretations give our lives a sense of security and comfort, providing the illusion of living well because we are doing what everyone else does (BT, 223). In short, our understanding of things is mediated by the world into which we are thrown. The problem today is that we are thrown into a worldview of global machination, a worldview that is totalizing insofar as it "blocks off" or "conceals" any other way to interpret beings, including ourselves (QCT, 33). To this end, the present age "masters" us to the extent that we are forgetful of the historical values and "guiding determinations" that preceded it (BT, 43).

As mentioned earlier, Heidegger identifies three fundamental symptoms of modernity that signal the "darkening of the world and the destruction of the earth . . . *calculation, acceleration,* and *massiveness*" (CP, 83). Calculation is revealed in the way all things in the world are quantifiable and organized in terms of instrumental principles. Through the lens of calculation, the mountain stream shows up as acre-feet of water, the forest as board-feet of lumber, and an office building full of human beings is quantified as "human resources." In the technological age, all things are subject to the governing rules of calculation and "the incalculable is here only what has not yet been mastered by calculation." Thus calculation becomes the "basic law" of human behavior, where the organic rhythms of life are organized and compressed by "clock-time" with schedules and plans (CP, 84). With the ubiquity of the mechanical clock, the day is broken down in terms of the calculative productivity of hours, minutes, seconds, and, today, even tenths of seconds.

The classical sociology of Karl Marx, Max Weber, and Emil Durkheim had anticipated Heidegger's critique by engaging the phenomenon of clock-time and its adverse effects on modern social life. Marx, for instance, revealed how the manipulation and exploitation of time as a measurable commodity is fundamental to the machinery of capitalism, forcing the working class into longer, more intense, and competitive workdays that tore at the fabric of social life and strained physical reserves.[4] Weber showed how the emergence of the clock and the rise of capitalism resonated to an increasingly disciplined

Protestant work ethic in Europe and America, where the wasting of time became the most serious of sins.

> Waste of time is thus the first and in principle the deadli-
> est of sins. The span of human life is infinitely short and
> precious to make sure of one's own election. Loss of time
> through sociability, idle talk, luxury, even more sleep than
> is necessary to health . . . is worthy of absolute moral con-
> demnation.[5]

Durkheim addressed the more extreme consequences of a life increasingly regulated by the impersonal structures of clock-time, which
resulted in the fragmentation of stabilizing social norms. In his 1897
essay "La Suicide," he suggested that it was on the basis of instrumental socioeconomic changes in the industrial age that an earlier
sense of communal belongingness and social integration was being
destroyed, creating an underlying sense of anomie and loneliness that
increasingly ends in suicide.[6]

Following the lead of these early social theorists, Heidegger
explored how life on the clock creates the phenomenon of acceleration.
For Heidegger, acceleration captures the ways in which our everyday
life involves a relation to speed, a frenzied tempo or "mania" embodied in the current tendency of "not-being-able-to-bear the stillness"
(CP, 84). This mania is exhibited in everyday body comportments
that are shaped by what social psychologist Robert Levine calls "time
urgency." Levine suggests the accelerated self can be identified as one
who continually glances at his or her watch and checks his or her
cell phone and e-mail; speaks quickly and becomes frustrated when
someone takes too long to make a point; eats, walks, and drives fast
and becomes angry when caught in slow-moving traffic; is compul-
sively punctual and follows lists and schedules to manage his or her
day; and finds it difficult to wait in line or sit still without something
or someone to distract or occupy him or her.[7]

As a consequence, acceleration reveals a unique relation to time.
In my everyday life, I am captivated with or "entranced" by the things
I am dealing with "now." For Heidegger, living in the now leaves
me in a constant state of "limbo" because I am unable to ask how or
why I am captivated with particular things and where this captivation
might take me (FCM, 120). Heidegger writes:

> [This] letting oneself go with whatever is happening around
> us is possible only if, from the outset, we constantly let

whatever is going on come toward us, come *up against us*, just as it is given. It is possible only if *we are entirely present* [*ganz Gegenwart*] in the face of whatever is happening around us, or, as we say, only if we simply make present [*gegenwärtigen*]. (FCM, 124)

As we saw earlier, being caught up in the "present" (*Gegenwart*) cuts me off from an authentic awareness of what Heidegger calls "primordial temporality."[8] To the extent that the accelerated self is absorbed in the "now" of clock-time, I forget how my life is shaped by the past and the future, by the temporal structures of "situatedness" (*Befindlichkeit*) and "projection" (*Entwurf*). Again, situatedness refers to the past insofar as I am always already thrown into a sociohistorical situation that determines how things affect me in terms of certain temperaments or moods. And projection refers to the future insofar as I am always "ahead-of-[my]self" (*sich vorweg*) as I ceaselessly press forward into possibilities, into already available social roles, practices, and identities, until my greatest own-most (*eigenst*) possibility, death. Busily captivated by the present, I forget that I am a "thrown project"; I forget the past and the future, that is, where my everyday self- interpretation comes from and where it is heading.

To this end, the symptom of acceleration reveals a self that is increasingly harried and fragmented insofar as it is pulled apart by competing commitments and investments that are always, for some reason, urgent. Ironically, this kind of fragmentation can often be experienced most intensely on days of "leisure." As I wake up on a sunny Saturday morning, I have no obligation to go to the office but I am still pulled into the "now" as a jumble of pressing possibilities. I *must* wash the car, mow the lawn, pick up the dry cleaning, check my e-mail, go for a jog, buy groceries, pay the bills, and if I finish these tasks I can watch the football game in the evening. By day's end, I am not relaxed and contented but exhausted, wondering where the day went. Thus as Kenneth Gergen points out, the paradox of accelerated living is that it does not result in exhilarating satisfaction but often a feeling of being defeated and overwhelmed.[9] We can get a clearer sense of this experience by looking at Heidegger's discussion of "handiness" in *Being and Time*.

As we saw in chapter 1, prior to any detached theorizing about the objective properties and characteristics of things, we are already involved with a "handy" (*zuhanden*) nexus of intraworldly equipment. To this end, the equipment that I handle in my everyday activities is never understood in isolation: "taken strictly, there 'is' no such thing as *an* equipment" (BT, 97). Equipment is always "something-in-order-to," already directed toward some particular task and always belonging to a nexus of other equipment.

> Equipment—in accordance with its equipmentality—always is in terms of its belonging to other equipment: inkstand, pen, ink, paper, blotting pad, table, lamp, furniture, windows, doors, room. (BT, 97)

When I use equipment in my everyday dealings, I embody a prereflective understanding or familiarity with my worldly context. In this regard, I am not a disembodied subject theoretically set over and against objects; rather, in my practical dealing, I am holistically interwoven to things in the activity of the work itself. I understand things insofar as I prereflectively handle, manipulate, and use them. A hammer, for instance, comes into being for me *as* a hammer as I use it "in-order-to-hammer."

> The less we [theoretically] stare at the hammer-thing, and the more we seize hold of it and use it, the more primordial does our relationship to it become, and the more unveiledly is it encountered as *that which it is*—as equipment. (BT, 98, emphasis added)

And when things are working smoothly in our workaday lives, the equipment that I use—doors, pens, computer keyboards, coffee cups—tend to withdraw or become "transparent." When I am engaged in the world, I am not thematically aware of the various tools I am using. Heidegger explains:

> The ready-to-hand is not grasped theoretically at all. . . . The peculiarity of what is proximally ready-to-hand is that, in readiness-to-hand, it must, as it were withdraw [*zurück-zuziehen*] in order to be ready-to-hand. . . . That with which our everyday dealing proximally dwells is not the tools themselves. On the contrary, that with which we concern ourselves primarily is the world. (BT, 99)

It is only when there is a breakdown or disturbance in the interconnected flow of my everyday life that I become thematically conscious of the tool as an object that is separate and distinct from me.

Although Heidegger does not explicitly explore the problem, the same can be said of the body. Like the tools that surround me, my body is always already usefully employed in daily activities. I use my hand prereflectively as a tool to open the door, type on the computer, answer the phone, or wave to someone across campus. My hand also does not perform its tasks in isolation. In the same way the computer is connected to a larger totality, to a printer, a phone, a desk, and a coffee mug, my hand belongs to a larger totality, connected to my arm, shoulder, chest, torso, and my entire perceptual horizon. Finally, in my daily routines, my body takes on the same type of mindless "transparency" when it is functioning smoothly. I do not notice my legs and arms as I walk down the hall carrying my briefcase in the same way that I do not notice the computer as I use it to type up my notes. Tools and body have a tendency to withdraw in their everyday use.[10]

Hans-Georg Gadamer interprets this smooth, transparent state of embodied agency in terms of "health."

> So what possibilities stand before us when we are consider-
> ing the question of health? Without doubt it is part of our
> nature as living beings that our conscious self-awareness
> remains largely in the background so that our enjoyment of
> good health is constantly concealed from us. Yet despite its
> hidden character health none the less manifests itself in a
> general feeling of well-being. It shows itself above all where
> such a feeling of well-being means we are open to new
> things, ready to embark on new enterprises, and forgetful
> of ourselves, scarcely notic[ing] the demands and strains
> which are put on us. This is what health is.[11]

What Gadamer is suggesting is that when we are rhythmically engaged in our workaday routines, our bodies, like tools, are concealed from us. Health, in this regard, is not to be understood as an experience that is felt inside one's corporeal body. It is a reference to how we are seamlessly woven into the world, where intraworldly things—including our bodies fit together and make sense in a smooth, inconspicuous way. Gadamer continues:

> Health is not a condition that one introspectively feels in
> oneself. Rather, it is a condition of being there (Da-sein),
> of being in the word, of being together with one's fellow

> human beings, of active rewarding engagement in one's
> everyday tasks. . . . It is the rhythm of life, a permanent
> process in which equilibrium reestablishes itself. This is
> something known to us all. Think of the processes of
> breathing, digesting, and sleeping.[12]

However, just as the tool reveals itself as a conspicuous object when
there is a breakdown or malfunction in the rhythmic flow of everydayness, the body also reveals itself as an object when the flow is
disrupted. Today, this experience of breakdown is increasingly facili-
tated by the unique velocity of technological existence as it becomes
more difficult for the body to adapt to the harried rhythms of a life
controlled and regulated by machines. In the modern city, we are
constantly being compelled toward speed, punctuality, and being
"on time." The consequence is a heightened state of nervous arousal,
physical stress, and overstimulation rooted in a need to go faster, to
do more things in less time, and this can lead to a breakdown of our
embodied connection with the world.[13] The smooth bodily processes
that are ordinarily inconspicuous emerge as objectlike; our breathing
becomes difficult; digestion is interrupted; the back and neck are
tightened; nervousness increases; and deep sleep is unreachable.

This experience of bodily breakdown is prompted by what
cardiac psychologists Diane Ulmer and Leonard Schwartzburd call
"hurry sickness," referring to a self that suffers from "severe and
chronic feelings of time urgency that have brought about changes
affecting personality and lifestyle."[14] The self is caught in a repeating
cycle of behavior, a "time pathology" that nervously hungers for more
things, more distractions, and interprets his or her self-worth in terms
of quantitative accomplishments and the accumulation of material
goods. Drawing on over two decades of clinical experience, Ulmer
and Schwartzburd identify three areas in which acceleration affects the
self in detrimental ways. First, in terms of physical health, the experience of time pressure and chronic sensory arousal contributes to the
proliferation of heart disease, high blood pressure, obesity, emotional
fatigue, insomnia, and increasing tendencies toward hostility and rage.
Second, in a social or interpersonal sense, acceleration contributes to
the fragmentation of relationships and the emotional support systems
of family and friends that take time to develop and sustain, leading
to an increasing sense of isolation and loneliness. Finally, on a psychological level, Ulmer and Schwartzburd identify a general mental
state associated with acceleration that has "received little attention in
the empirical literature," a mood described as

a personal, perhaps even spiritual, barrenness or emptiness
spawned by the chronic struggle to accomplish tasks, which
can lead to a rather joyless existence and give rise to covert
self-destructive behaviors.[15]

According to Heidegger, the accelerated self is, quite simply, suffering
from "boredom" (*Langeweile*). Thrown into a harried world, we are
so restless, so sped up, that we become indifferent, unable to qualitatively distinguish which choices, commitments, and obligations are
significant or matter to us.

Acceleration and Boredom

Georg Simmel, in his influential 1903 essay "The Metropolis and Mental
Life," sets the stage for Heidegger's observations. According to Simmel, the intense stimulation of the nervous system in modern cities
invariably leads to a temperament that is fundamentally "blasé."

> Through the mere quantitative intensification of the same
> conditioning factors this achievement is transformed into its
> opposite and appears in the peculiar adjustment of the blasé
> attitude. In this phenomenon the nerves find in the refusal
> to react to their stimulation in the last possibility of accom-
> modating to the contents and forms of metropolitan life.[16]

For Simmel, the nervous system of the metropolitan subject—bom-
barded by increasingly diverse stimuli—invariably reaches a peak of
overstimulation and the body responds, out of sheer "self-preserva-
tion," by relying on the intellect, "a protective organ" that is rooted
in emotional detachment.

> The metropolitan type of man . . . develops an organ protect-
> ing him against the threatening currents and discrepancies
> of his external environment which would uproot him. He
> reacts with his head instead of his heart.[17]

This intellectual detachment has both a positive and negative function. Positively, because it is the "least sensitive" part of the psyche,
the intellect provides a self-preserving emotional barrier, anesthetizing
the subject from the sensory "shocks and inner upheavals" that are
symptomatic of metropolitan life. Negatively, it results in a life that

is based not on personal and emotional connections to the world but on instrumental "logical operations."[18] The consequence of this type of calculative individualization is, for Simmel, boredom, a disengaged indifference to one's everyday choices and commitments.

Boredom, in this regard, emerges insidiously as we are busily occupied with our workaday routines. It is on the basis of our harried busy-ness that we have difficulty responding qualitatively to the various tasks and projects in which we are engaged. In short, it is modern life itself that "makes [us bored], because it agitates the nerves to their strongest reactivity for such a long time that they finally cease to react at all."[19] The result is an inability to distinguish which activity actually matters to us, creating a "devaluation of the whole objective world, a devaluation which in the end unavoidably drags one's own personality down into a feeling of the same worthlessness."[20] If family obligations, work, exercise, shopping, and dining must all be efficiently performed within an increasingly compressed schedule, then it becomes difficult to identify which of these activities is more meaningful or significant than the others. In our heightened state of nervous indifference, all of our choices take on an equal significance; we do not have a strong emotional reaction to any of them. Things, says Simmel, begin to appear in "an evenly flat and gray tone, [where] no one object deserves preference over any other."[21] Accelerated existence, therefore, begins to exercise a tacit but an elemental control over us, carrying us along with little or no conscious awareness of what is going on, "as if in a stream, and one needs hardly to swim for oneself."[22]

Heidegger deepens Simmel's analysis in his 1929–30 Freiburg lecture course "The Fundamental Concepts of Metaphysics"[23] by distinguishing between three kinds of boredom, "becoming bored *by* something" (*Gelangweiltwerden von etwas*), "being bored *with* something" (*Sichlangweilen bei etwas*), and "being bored" (*Sichlangweilen*) itself.[24] The first kind of boredom is the ordinary conception, referring to how I encounter or find certain things or situations. For instance, I may "become bored *by*" a particular book, a long drive, or waiting for a flight in the airport. Indeed, I can even find myself boring. When I am bored by something, I feel "empty," "indifferent," and "depressed," and I must find a way to "while" away the time (FCM, 79).[25] This feeling of indifference is "conspicuous" insofar as it has an object; I am bored *by* such and such. Consequently, this form of boredom is "halting" or transient insofar as it comes and goes in my life. For instance, once my plane takes off after waiting in the airport, I am no longer bored. To this end, "what is boring comes from outside. . . . A *particular* situation with *its* circumstances *transposes us* into boredom" (FCM, 128).

This kind of conspicuous boredom is contrasted with a second, more profound kind. "Being bored *with* something" is less obtrusive than the first kind of boredom, because it emerges when I make no effort to "while away" the time. Heidegger gives the example of a dinner party filled with good food, music, and conversation. At the party, I do not notice myself "killing time" because I am caught up in the "now," in the activities and gossip of the social event. When I am absorbed in these kinds of public pastimes, it is difficult for me to notice my own boredom. In the shared moment, I am doing—eating, drinking, laughing, singing—what "anyone" (*das Man*) and everyone does. Thus this type of boredom remains hidden and inconspicuous. It is, as Heidegger says, "admittedly hard to find, and this is precisely because it presents itself in a public manner" (FCM, 112). Indeed, it is only after I return home that I realize I was bored the whole time, yet I cannot point to a particular conspicuous thing that made the party boring. The party *as a whole* was boring. It just took up time. Hence, this more profound kind of boredom does not refer to the way we encounter particular things. Rather, it arises inconspicuously in our involvement in certain public situations, therefore, "it does not come from outside: *it arises from out of Dasein itself*" (FCM, 128).

Although the second form of boredom is more primordial than the first, to the extent that it conceals itself, it is similar to the first form, insofar as it is situational; it lingers for a while and then goes away. This is to be contrasted with the third, most profound kind of boredom, one that is no longer situational but refers to the mood of the modern world itself, the entire sociohistorical horizon in which we are currently involved. Heidegger says "being bored" or "profound boredom" (*tiefe Langeweile*) designates that "*it is boring for one.*" The "It" (*Es*), in this case, is the totality of relations that make up the world; it is "*beings as a whole*" (FCM, 134, 138). Profound boredom, in this regard, is not transient; it does not come and go but rather captures the fact that the world itself is boring, and "everyone" is bored. In this regard, profound boredom does not refer to my own private, emotional states that are affected by a conspicuous thing or an inconspicuous situation. In profound boredom, "[we are] *elevated beyond* the *particular situation* in each case and beyond the *specific beings* surrounding us" (FCM, 137). Profound boredom, therefore, is regarded as a structural feature of modern existence itself, a characteristic of our "situatedness" (*Befindlichkeit*).

Again, situatedness, our "where-we're-at-ness,"[26] refers to the way in which we find ourselves invariably thrown into a shared world that attunes or affects us in terms of public "moods" (*Stimmung*). Because I always find myself in a situation that matters to me, I am already "attuned," already in a mood (BT, 176–77). This means boredom is not in *me*; boredom is already "there." As a fundamental attunement or "ground-mood" (*Grund-Stimmung*), profound boredom refers to an ontological condition that attunes the accelerated self in the technological age, a self that continually seeks to be filled up with things and is immersed or "swept away" in "whatever is going on or happening around [it]" (FCM, 124).

Profound boredom becomes ubiquitous because all I do is "pass the time" with the various things that occupy and consume me during the day. My whole life is organized and managed in terms of busily "driving away whatever is boring" by filling up an underlying feeling of indifference or emptiness through constant activity: working, eating out, exercising, traveling, and shopping. Heidegger refers to activity that is endlessly dispersed in the production and consumption of things as "self-forming *emptiness*" (FCM, 126). The historian of psychology, Philip Cushman, agrees with Heidegger, describing the "empty self" as one

> [who] seeks the experience of being continually filled up by consuming goods, calories, experiences, politicians, romantic partners, and empathic therapists in an attempt to combat the growing alienation and fragmentation of its era. [It] is dependent on the continual consumption of nonessential and quickly obsolete items or experiences . . . accomplished through the dual creation of easy credit and a gnawing sense of emptiness in the self.[27]

According to Heidegger, the empty self is anyone and everyone, and because it is so pervasive, our own emptiness remains hidden from us; it is, as Heidegger says, "peculiarly inconspicuous" (FCM, 127).

The modern self, therefore, does not even know that it is bored, because it has grown into a temperament of boredom. This makes profound boredom doubly oppressive. Initially, the frantic pace of modern life makes it increasingly difficult for us to distinguish which choices and commitments actually matter to us in our lives. And when we cannot distinguish what matters, we become indifferent. Everything is equally important, because nothing stands out, nothing matters. "In this ennui," says Heidegger, "nothing appeals to us anymore; everything has as much or as little value as everything else, because a deep boredom penetrates our existence to the core."[28] Yet on a more profound level, we are oblivious to our own indifference, because this is what it means *to be* in the modern world.

> [Because] what is boring is here diffused throughout the par-
> ticular situation as a whole, it is far more oppressive—despite
> its ungraspability. It oppresses in and during the inconspicu-
> ous way in which we are held at a distance in our passing
> the time. (FCM, 128)

As a result, the more profound the boredom, "the more silent, the less public, the quieter, the more inconspicuous, and wide-ranging it is" (FCM, 134). And the boredom of the technological age has become so powerful, so pervasive, that the accelerated self "no longer has any power [against it]" (FCM, 136). When the world *as a whole* shows up as a totality of instrumental things to be consumed, produced, and exchanged in order to "pass the time," then everything is swallowed by indifference, including human beings.

> All of the sudden everything is enveloped and embraced
> by this indifference. Beings have—as we say—become indif-
> ferent *as a whole*, and we ourselves as these people are not
> excepted. (FCM, 138)

This totalizing aspect of profound boredom points to the third symptom of the present age, "the outbreak of massiveness." In *Contributions*, Heidegger suggests that the accelerated self has become enfeebled, because "the unfettered hold of the frenzy of the gigantic has over- whelmed him under the guise of 'magnitude' " (CP, 6). We are now living in the reign of "the gigantic" (*das Riesenhafte*). The world emerges as a global network of compressed, hyper-fast relations that constantly pull us "everywhere and nowhere all at once, [where] everything gets lumped together into a uniform distancelessness" (TT, 163–64).

Today, the accelerated self is "bewitched, dazzled, and beguiled" by the total domination of the gigantic, soothed by the frenzy of usable, consumable beings (DT, 56). Heidegger suggests the reign of the gigantic is one where we are all in a state of restless "enchant- ment" with beings to the point that we can no longer protect ourselves from enchantment.

One has only to know from where the enchantment comes. The answer: from the unrestrained domination of machination. When machination finally dominates and permeates everything, then there are no longer any conditions by which to detect the enchantment and to protect oneself from it. (CP, 86–87)

Thus enchantment with beings—rooted in calculative and accelerated ways of being—comes "to be accepted and practiced *as the only way*" of being (DT, 56). It is for this reason that the accelerated self is in danger of living a fundamentally barren life, one that pathologically seeks to fill an underlying emptiness. This is precisely why, as Cushman writes, the frantic cycles of consumption continue.

This is a powerful illusion. And what fuels the illusion, what impels the individual into this illusion, is the desperation to fill up the empty self. . . . It must consume in order to be soothed and integrated; it must "take in" and merge with a self-object celebrity, an ideology, or a drug, or it will be in danger of fragmenting into feelings of worthlessness and confusion.[29]

The situation is particularly troubling if we understand that mainstream health professions largely overlook the social and historical conditions that create this modern sense of fragmentation and emptiness by uncritically adopting the disengaged and mechanistic perspective of the natural sciences.

In this regard, Heidegger's project makes a significant contribution to the study of health and illness, specifically by opening up ways to reenvision therapy. For Heidegger, the primary focus of therapy should not be on "what" the patient is as an objective, material thing (*Körper*) but on "how" the patient lives in terms of his or her embodied involvement (*Leib*) in the world. Indeed, by the early 1940s, Heidegger's existential analytic had inspired a new movement in the mental health professions called "*Daseinsanalyse.*" Prominent psychiatrists and psychologists such as Ludwig Binswanger, Medard Boss, and Ronald Kuhn—disenchanted with the reductive, scientific theories that were dominating the profession—turned to Heidegger's analysis of human existence for guidance. Binswanger explains how this approach departs from the prevailing scientific worldview.

A psychotherapy on existential-analytic bases investigates the life-history of the patient to be treated, . . . but it does not explain this life-history and its pathologic idiosyncrasies according to the teachings of any school of psychotherapy, or by means of its preferred categories. Instead, it *understands* [*Verstehen*] this life-history as modifications of the total structure of the patient's being-in-the-world.[30]

By paying attention to the "life-history" of the patient, *Daseinsanalyse* not only situates the patient "there" (*Da*), unfolding in a particular time and place, but it also reveals how the "there" already shapes the assumptions and practices of psychotherapy itself. In this regard, it is precisely because mechanistic and biological approaches to health and illness overlook the accelerated historical situation of the patient that mainstream psychotherapy may be perpetuating the patterns of behavior that manifest the patient's boredom and nervousness in the first place. This dilemma needs to be explored further.

Acceleration and Psychotherapy

Understood as "the science of mental processes and human behavior," the discipline of psychology is a historical outgrowth of the eighteenth-century paradigm of the natural sciences in two fundamental ways. First, psychology is concerned with a specific "method" or procedure based on the observation of material objects in causal interaction, interaction that can be empirically tested and systematically quantified, resulting in the discovery of general laws. In this regard, modern psychology attempts to reduce behavior to elemental causes that are measurable, testable, and repeatable. Indeed, as Bertrand Russell suggests, one of the goals of psychology was to develop "a mathematics of human behavior as precise as the mathematics of machines."[31] Second, psychology seeks a perspective of detached objectivity, what Thomas Nagel calls a "view from nowhere," which is free from the distortions and misleading assumptions of everyday life.[32] This disengaged perspective downplays the fact that our emotional well-being is largely shaped by a concrete social and historical context, focusing instead on the physical pathology of the individual. From this standpoint, psychology is left with a very narrow approach to therapy, one that is concerned with "repairing damage within a disease model of human functioning."[33]

In his Zollikon seminars, Heidegger maintains that all of the various manifestations of modern psychology, including psychoanalysis, are held under "the dictatorship" of the scientific method that reduces human behavior to elemental causal interactions and views emotional suffering from the perspective of detached objectivity (ZS, 17–18, 186, 233). Freud confirms Heidegger's criticism when he claims that "psychoanalysis *must* accept the scientific *Weltanshauung*" because

> the intellect and the mind are objects for scientific research
> in exactly the same way as non-human beings. . . . Our best
> hope for the future is that intellect—the scientific spirit,
> reason—may in the process of time establish a dictatorship
> in the mental life of man.[34]

Today, the "scientific spirit" has emerged as psychopharmacology, which has replaced psychoanalysis as the dominant therapeutic model. Based on this view, the psychiatrist invariably refers to the latest version of the *Diagnostic and Statistical Manual of Mental Disorders* (DSM, IV), a document that catalogues a massive list of observable pathologies, identifies various symptoms, and prescribes ways in which to treat the causes of these symptoms. A client, for instance, with observable symptoms of depression is prescribed medication in order to fix the biologically determined cause, specifically, the chemical levels of serotonin and dopamine in the brain. The medication will balance these levels, block out the feelings of depression and emptiness, and allow the client to effectively and functionally reenter his or her rapid-paced world. This approach to therapy is problematic.

First of all, psychopharmacology, like psychoanalysis, presupposes a conception of the self that is, in no way, transhistorical. It is a conception rooted in uniquely modern assumptions of individualism and causal determinism. The therapist interprets the client as an encapsulated thing or object that needs to be fixed by instrumental techniques and fails to address the underlying sociohistorical etiology that may be contributing to the client's disorder. Furthermore, the therapist interprets the mental health of the client largely in terms of his or her competence in handling the frantic pace of modern life, and this has a tendency to perpetuate the very social conditions that manifested the feelings of indifference and emptiness in the first place.[35] In short, by ignoring the fact that the practice of psychotherapy itself and the emotional conditions that it treats are shaped by our involvement in a particular social and historical situation, our own emptiness, as Heidegger says, continues to remain hidden from us (FCM, 164).

Indeed, it can be argued that many of the newest illnesses in the latest *DSM* are a direct result of accelerated social conditions. Among these we might include: (1) the most ubiquitous anxiety disorders mediated by chronic sensory arousal and time pressure—such as "panic disorder," "generalized anxiety disorder," and "social phobia"; (2) personality disorders perpetuated by a culture that values rapid multitasking and racing thought patterns—such as "obsessive-compulsive personality disorder" and "attention deficit/hyperactivity disorder"; and (3) impulse disorders based on socially determined expectations of instant satisfaction or gratification—such as "pathological gambling and shopping disorder," "kleptomania," and "intermittent explosive disorder." The mechanistic approach to curing these illnesses results in a paradox if what is causing the disorder is itself an accelerated, mechanized way of living.

The way therapy is provided today illustrates this paradox. With market forces and health management organizations (HMOs) imposing time restraints on patient visits, today's therapeutic sessions are increasingly compressed and mediated by assumptions of efficiency and cost-effectiveness, where the therapist is there to either quickly teach the client cognitive-behavioral techniques or prescribe and refill medication. Thus by overlooking the way in which the practice of psychotherapy itself is shaped by an accelerated world, therapists have not only been treating the accelerated self, they have, according to Cushman, "also been constructing it, profiting from it, and not challenging the social arrangement that created it."[36]

Even alternative forms of therapy that do not focus on the pathological condition of the client fail to articulate the fundamental role that our sociohistorical situation plays in determining emotional well-being. Charles Guignon's recent critique of the renewed interest in positive psychology is a case in point.[37] Positive psychology is defined as "a science of positive subjective experience, positive individual traits, and positive institutions [that] promises to improve the quality of life and prevent the pathologies that arise when life is barren and meaningless."[38] To this end, positive psychology does not address the observable symptoms of the disorder. Rather, it embraces the active agency of the client who now focuses his or her energies not on the dark moods of emptiness and ennui but on the positive and optimistic qualities of life, even if such qualities are simply illusions. "One of the most impressive findings . . . of positive psychology," says Guignon, "is that positive illusions and unrealistic optimism are in fact beneficial to people, helping them cope with stressful events and extending their lives."[39] This refocusing on positive illusions will allow the client to interpret himself or herself as a "decision maker with choices, preferences, and the possibility of becoming masterful [and] efficacious."[40]

What remains problematic is that the optimistic values promoted by positive psychology are not timeless; they are themselves products of a technological economy aimed at efficacy and quick fixes. For instance, as Guignon points out, the client does not embrace the positive virtues of Aristotle's *Nicomachean Ethics* such as shame, wittiness, pride, and courage, nor does he or she focus on the Judeo-Christian virtues of humility, selflessness, and meekness.[41] Rather, the psychotherapist asks the client to focus on uniquely modern values that accommodate the interpretation of the self that psychology inherits from Cartesian and empiricist epistemologies. Thus the self is interpreted as an enclosed, masterful, autonomous subject that can manipulate and effectively control surrounding objects. This leads the client of positive psychology to focus on values such as "self-determination,"[42] "adaptability,"[43] "creativity,"[44] and "individual happiness."[45]

In doing so, the now optimistic and self-assertive client will be empowered, able to master the accelerated work world as an effective and optimally functioning individual. The upshot of this is that the therapist fails to acknowledge the fact that the client's positive values are themselves socially and historically constructed. This results in a twofold dilemma. First, the therapist overlooks the possibility of older, alternative virtues that are part of our shared history, such as communal belongingness, attachment, and dependency, in favor of ultramodern individualism and autonomy. The therapist, therefore, is unable to address the client's experience of isolation and emptiness because the client continues to interpret himself or herself as a self-reliant subject who is cut off from the world rather than someone who belongs to it. Furthermore, by uncritically adopting the values of a technological economy, positive psychology reinforces the same instrumental, accelerated way of living that initially brought about the client's feelings of emptiness.

To this end, Heidegger's project reveals how the health professions continue to "misinterpret" the self as either a masterful, subjective consciousness or a quantifiable, causally determined object (ZS, 272). For Heidegger, medicine is called to acknowledge the ontological fact that the self is always already "being-in-the-world," and it is this ongoing involvement in the world that makes possible the modern interpretation of the self. This is why understanding human existence in terms of Dasein can be so helpful to health professionals. With Heidegger, the world is not interpreted as a container filled with objects within which the self resides. Rather, it is a meaningful nexus of social relations, and the self is already concretely involved with and embedded in this nexus. As Heidegger says,

> Self and world belong together in the single entity, the Dasein. Self and world are not two beings, like subject

and object, or I and thou, but self and world are the basic determination of the Dasein itself in the unity of the structure of being-in-the-world. (BP, 297)

By dismantling the philosophical assumptions of the modern worldview, Heidegger shows us how the practice of psychotherapy can be enhanced by focusing on the sociohistorical aspect of the manifestation of individual pathologies. Mainstream psychiatry and psychology, in this regard, do not discover timeless principles of human behavior. The therapeutic practice of psychology itself is a historical phenomenon, the result of an increasingly accelerated, mechanized, and individualistic way of life that began to take hold in the late nineteenth century, a way of life that brought with it its own brand of emotional malaise. Turn-of-the-century philosophers and social theorists such as Heidegger responded to this cultural transformation by introducing and redefining terms—such as *anxiety* (Kierkegaard), *boredom* (Simmel), *alienation* (Marx), *disenchantment* (Weber), the *mass man* (Ortega y Gasset), and *anomie* (Durkheim)—in order to engage these emerging pathologies. Thus in order to properly understand the self, the health professions must come to grips with the movement of history that shapes the understanding of who we are. Indeed, "to understand history," as Heidegger reminds us, "cannot mean anything else than to understand ourselves" (PS, 7).

We can summarize Heidegger's contribution to the health professions in the following way. First, Heidegger reveals how the frenzied pace of technological life embodies a "hidden distress" in the inconspicuous cultural mood of boredom. By emphasizing a standpoint of detached objectivity, mainstream psychiatry and psychology largely overlook the social forms that manifest this shared feeling of indifference and fail to recognize the ways in which the modern self drives away this indifference with the frantic consumption and production of goods and services. This disengaged perspective makes it all but impossible for psychologists and psychiatrists to recognize how they participate in the construction of the accelerated self.

Second, by remaining attentive to how our everyday understanding of things and our moods and dispositions are always already mediated by a sociohistorical situation, Heidegger deconstructs the modern conception of the self as an autonomous subject or a biologically determined object. He, therefore, undermines the traditional interpretation of the detached doctor who neutrally examines the objective symptoms of the patient. By uncritically adopting this interpretation, mainstream biomedicine largely neglects the concrete situation that is already there, shaping the emotional state and comportment of patient and physician alike. Heidegger reveals that the doctor is, first and foremost, not a disengaged spectator but a "being-in-the-world," pretheoretically involved in the public practices and assumptions of modernity.

Finally, and perhaps most importantly, Heidegger's project opens up the possibility for health professionals to broaden their approach to treatment by incorporating a wide-ranging historical and cultural understanding of individual pathologies. This understanding enables the physician to break free from what Heidegger calls "scientism," where science is dogmatically accepted as "the new religion" insofar as its method alone can provide us with *the* objective truth about illness and suffering (ZS, 18). In his Zollikon seminars, Heidegger explains:

> Science is, to an almost incredible degree, dogmatic everywhere, that is, it operates with preconceptions and prejudices which have not been reflected on. There is the highest need for doctors who think and do not wish to leave the field entirely to the scientific technicians. (ZS, 103)

By regarding the human being as "an object which is present-at-hand," mainstream medicine ignores our ontological character, that prior to any objectification, we are a finite, sociohistorical *way of being*, a way of being that opens up the Da-sein, the "clearing" or "there" that makes possible any worldview—scientific or otherwise. Heidegger's hermeneutic approach reveals the extent to which science is always already grounded in an unfolding historical horizon. Such an approach can release the doctor from the dogmatic prejudices of the scientific method and release the patient from an increasingly narrow definition of the self that is rooted in modern assumptions of individualism, self-reliance, and busy-ness. It is largely on the basis of these assumptions, after all, that the contemporary experiences of isolation and nervous indifference manifest, leading so many into the doctor's office in the first place.

Acknowledging the fact that we have been thrown into acceleration, we can now turn our attention to Heidegger's thoughts on the possibility of releasing ourselves from it by recovering ways of being that are more leisurely and playful. This recovery, as we will see, has the potential to free us from the harried routines and practices of the technological work world and gives us an opening to face the abyssal nature of our own being and the mystery that "beings are" in the first place. In the final chapter, we will explore the possibility that genuine leisure may reconnect us to "wonder" (*Erstaunen*) as the original temperament of Western thought. In wonder, we do not seek to instrumentally control and master beings but calmly accept the unsettledness of being and are, as a result, allowed into the awesome openness or "event" (*Ereignis*) that lets beings emerge on their own terms.

Recovering Play

On Authenticity and Dwelling

Today we uncritically embrace the values of the technological work world: speed, efficiency, usefulness, and productivity. However, looking back just a few hundred years to preindustrial Europe reveals an entirely different picture concerning our relationship between work and leisure. Thomas Anderson explains the difference:

> In Medieval Europe, holidays, holy days, took up one-third of the year in England, almost five months of the year in Spain—even for peasants. Although work was from sunrise to sunset, it was casual, able to be interrupted for a chat with a friend, a long lunch, a visit to the pub or the fishing hole—none of which a modern factory office worker dare do. The fact is that American workers of the mid-twentieth century with their 40-hour week were just catching up with medieval counterparts; and American workers at the end of this century have fallen behind their medieval ancestors! Our incredible growth in technology has not resulted in a corresponding increase in leisure.[1]

In this concluding chapter, I explore this contemporary loss of leisure in light of Heidegger's conception of authentic dwelling. I suggest that the premodern conception of leisure may provide a link that unifies, what appear to be, conflicting versions of Heidegger's notion of authenticity. Authenticity in *Being and Time* is commonly interpreted in terms of willful commitment and "resoluteness" (*Entschlossenheit*) in the face of one's own death but is, by the late 1930s, reintroduced in terms of *Gelassenheit*, as a nonwillful way of dwelling that is open to the enigmatic emerging forth of beings, an openness that "lets beings be." I argue that in *Being and Time*, authenticity is not, at its deepest

127

level, to be interpreted in "existentialist" terms, as a way of being that individualizes the self, that severs ties to the world and allows the subject to confront his or her own finitude and take future action on the basis of this confrontation. For Heidegger, to be authentic is to own up to one's being *as a whole*, and this means coming to grips not only with Dasein's future ("being-towards-death") but also with the communal past ("being-towards-the-beginning"). Authenticity, in this regard, involves a retrieval or "repetition" (*Wiederholung*) of Dasein's beginnings, what Heidegger calls authentic "historicality" (*Geschichtlichkeit*), referring to the cultural possibilities that belong to our shared history but have largely been forgotten, covered over by the conformist assumptions and prejudices of the modern world. By focusing on Heidegger's writings on Hölderlin in the 1930s and 1940s, I suggest that the ancient interpretation of leisure and festivity may play an important role in this historical retrieval.

Technology and Authentic Historicality

The technological age is violent, according to Heidegger, because it "sets upon" (*stellt*) nature and forces beings to show up or reveal themselves in *only one way*, as an object-region available for use. Caught up in the technological worldview, our lives have become increasingly frantic, sped up with machines and institutions that allow us to consume, produce, and exchange beings at faster rates. However, the suggestion that authenticity requires a temperament of slowness or tranquility is potentially misleading if we look at Heidegger's own remarks on "tranquility" (*Ruhe*) in *Being and Time*, where everyday busy-ness is itself understood as "tranquilizing" (*beruhigend*).

Again, our everyday interpretation of things is communal and is mediated in advance by the fast-paced technological world into which we are thrown. To this end, we all have an inveterate tendency to fall into a pregiven, public understanding that is comforting and familiar to the extent that we are doing what everyone else does. This tendency toward public conformism is, according to Heidegger, tranquilizing and is characterized in the modern age by three overlapping aspects: "idle talk" (*Gerede*), "curiosity" (*Neugier*), and "ambiguity" (*Zweideutigkeit*).

Heidegger describes idle talk as the way language or "discourse" (*Rede*) manifests itself in our everyday acts and practices. Based on this view, idle talk already "understands everything," because it is caught up in today's public interpretations, assumptions, and prejudices (BT, 212). In our turbo-capitalist world, for instance, idle talk has a tendency to circulate around the "very newest thing," the latest celebrity and political gossip, the fastest gadgets, the most productive and efficient worker, and it interprets what is newest, fastest, and most efficient in a positive light. Idle talk dovetails into curiosity, which captures the ways in which modern existence is restless, excitedly moving, traveling, and consuming as we search for the latest adventure and public novelty. In our restlessness, we are, all too often, "everywhere and nowhere" as we are pulled apart by competing commitments and distractions (BT, 217). And, because we are thrown into a common world, the things that we gossip about and are distracted by are the same things that anyone and everyone gossips about. This means that our everyday beliefs and choices are "ambiguous." Techno-scientific Dasein has already figured everything out, deciding in advance how we will interpret things and what we will believe in. Ambiguity, therefore, reveals how it has become increasingly difficult for us to come to grips with the unsettling, enigmatic aspects of being.

To be absorbed into the public world is soothing and tempting insofar as it disburdens us from having to face the difficult question of the meaning of our own being and convinces us that our choices and commitments are in "the best of order" because we are doing what everyone else does. Thus regardless of the fact that we are not calm and composed but "sucked into the turbulence" of *das Man* and convinced to "live at a faster rate," we are still tranquilized (BT, 222). We are "carried away" (*mitnehmen*) by the current fads and fashions (BT, 218). In order to address the possibility of an authentic response to public tranquilization we have to first dismantle the popularized, "existentialist" interpretation of Heideggerian authenticity.

As we saw earlier, Heidegger identifies the future as *the* primary temporal dimension of existence, a dimension embodied by our "projection" (*Entwurf*) into future possibilities. As such, the self should not be interpreted as a stable thing with a fixed identity—a wife, a lawyer, or a home owner—but as a "not yet" (*noch nicht*), a finite event that is always pressing forward, always on the way. Indeed, we become something, based on Heidegger's account, only when we *are* no longer. However, it is because we are tranquilized by everydayness, by the stabilizing assumptions, institutions, and routines of *das Man*, that we remain largely oblivious of the fact that our life, as being-towards-death, is fundamentally unsettled. In everydayness, our relationship to death is inauthentic to the extent that the public world is in denial, covering over a sincere awareness of our own finitude.

Authenticity, based on this existentialist reading, depends heavily on Heidegger's notion of "anxiety" (*Angst*), which is the mood that allegedly individuates us, making us self-determined by severing us from our comforting absorption in *das Man*. Anxiety makes it possible for us to clear-sightedly face the possibility of our own death, to be resolute as we anticipate our end rather than fleeing from it in our public routines. The authentic self is one who accepts anxiety and soberly acknowledges that any future action or decision must ultimately be made against the background of sheer nothingness. The ability to willfully disengage oneself from the familiar busy-ness of *das Man* is crucial based on this reading of authenticity, because " *'das Man' does not permit us the courage for anxiety in the face of death"* (BT, 298). This brand of authenticity has long been criticized for yielding a kind of extreme subjectivism or—as Heidegger's students Karl Löwith and Hans Jonas called it—"decisionism," where the level of commitment to one's own decisions in the face of nihilism is the sole measure of authenticity. The result, as Jonas suggests, is that "decision as such becomes the highest virtue."[2] I suggest that this existentialist interpretation of authenticity overemphasizes individuation and the futurity of existence and overlooks the crucial role that "historicality" (*Geschichtlichkeit*) and our "having-been-there" (*da-gewesen*) play in Heidegger's conception.

In the fifth chapter of the second division of *Being and Time*, Heidegger claims there is a "more radical" conception of authenticity, one that can be understood "in a way that is *more primordial* than in the projection of its authentic existence" (BT, 424, emphasis added). If authenticity involves owning up to one's being *as a whole*, then the account must recognize that being-towards-death is "just *one* of the ends by which Dasein's totality is closed around" (BT, 425).

> The other "end" is the "beginning," the "birth." Only that entity which is "between" birth and death presents the whole we have been seeking. Accordingly, the orientation of our analytic has so far remained "one sided," in spite of all its tendencies toward a consideration of existent being-a-whole and [in] spite of the genuineness with which authentic and inauthentic being-towards-death have been explicated. (BT, 425)

Heidegger refers to coming to grips with the beginning of Dasein as authentic historicality. It involves recovering the historical wellsprings or "sources" (*Ursprung*) that underlie our current understanding of being, sources that have been largely concealed and covered over by inauthentic busy-ness.[3] In order to properly understand the notion of authentic historicality, we must unpack Heidegger's distinction between "heritage" (*Erbe*) and "tradition" (*Tradition*).[4]

It is true that anxiety leaves us disoriented by disrupting our familiar ties to the institutions, assumptions, and norms of our tradition, but this does not mean that facing anxiety results in a solipsistic kind of authenticity, where the individual makes "resolute" (*entschlossen*) decisions against a background of nothingness. Because we are always already being-in-the-world, any decision or action that we take, whether authentic or inauthentic, is made possible by the historical culture into which we are thrown. Heidegger explains:

> Anxiety individualizes Dasein and thus discloses it as "*solus ipse*." But this existential "solipsism" is so far from the displacement of putting an isolated subject-thing into the innocuous emptiness of a worldless occurring, that in an extreme sense, what it does is precisely bring Dasein face to face with its world as world, and thus bring it face to face with itself as being-in-the-world. (BT, 233)

Dasein—as a historical *way of being*—stretches forward toward death *and* backward toward its beginning, and it is for this reason that anxiety never severs us wholly from *das Man*. Rather, it opens us up to the possibility of retrieving the common "heritage" (*Erbe*) that our current tradition conceals. Anxiety, based on this reading, is not individualizing; it actually opens up a deeper relationship with the world understood in terms of our shared history. Thus the individualistic reading of authenticity fails to the extent that it overemphasizes the self-determinative aspects of our being-towards-death and neglects the other direction of existence, our past, our being-towards-the-beginning.

Authenticity, on this view, has a twofold structure. Initially, it is to be understood in terms of being steadfast in the face of one's own death. More fundamentally, this decisiveness frees us from traditional assumptions and prejudices that today seek mastery and control over all things and reveals other, more original, historical and cultural possibilities. In this regard, it is helpful to rethink Heidegger's emphasis on courage, decisiveness, and, particularly, "resoluteness" (*Entschlossenheit*) in *Being and Time*, a term that, as Joan Stambaugh reminds us, contains within it the literal sense of "letting," "being unlocked," or "being open for something."[5] In his 1941 interpretation of Hölderlin's hymn "Remembrance" (*Andenken*), Heidegger makes this point explicit by revisiting core themes of authenticity not in terms of heroic decisiveness but in terms of "shyness" (*Scheuheit*). For Heidegger, shyness has nothing to do with being cowardly, bashful, or fainthearted. Shyness refers to the "expectant decisiveness to be patient . . . the courage to go slowly, a courage *decided long ago*" (RE, 153, emphasis added). In shyness, the authentic self does not impatiently manipulate things, forcing them to show up in a particular way but rather courageously "sets what is slow and patient on its way" (RE, 153). To this end, shyness is a recollection of a more original way of being that is open to beings and "lets beings be." Authentic historicality, in this regard, reminds us that the original temperament of shyness is already ours; it already belongs to the heritage of *das Man*. Authenticity, therefore, ultimately involves a reverence for and "repetition" (*Wiederholung*) of what has already been handed to us by our heritage.

> The resoluteness which comes back to itself and hands itself down, then becomes the repetition of a possibility of existence that has come back to us. Repeating is handing down explicitly—that is to say, going back into the possibilities of the Dasein that has-been-there. (BT, 437)

The question now becomes, what kind of embodied activity—in the wake of today's busy preoccupation with beings—lies in our heritage that can free us from traditional prejudices, and can such an activity be retrieved?

I want to suggest that clues might be found in uncovering the original meaning of leisure, an experience that cultivates a temperament more original than the dark dispositions of anxiety and boredom that, for Heidegger, are characteristic of the technological age. This other mood is "awe" or "wonder" (*Erstaunen*), and it can be recovered by staying attentive to our heritage. Wonder is a disposition that does not flee from the enigmatic event of being but celebrates it. It is here that Heidegger's notion of authenticity makes contact with the work of distinguished Thomist philosopher Josef Pieper and his influential analyses of leisure and festivity. This connection is worth exploring in more detail.[6]

Leisure and Openness to Mystery

In the summer of 1946 at the University of Münster, Pieper offered a course entitled "Defending Leisure: On Philosophical Education and Intellectual Work." This course led to the 1948 publication of his pioneering work *Leisure as the Basis of Culture*. In this book, Pieper challenges the modern cult of productivity and busy-ness, where the activity of leisure is interpreted as less important than "getting things done." Pieper, like Heidegger, sees workaday busy-ness as an inauthentic way of being, one that remains forever distracted by consuming and producing beings and flees from owning up to the unsettling question of the meaning of one's own life. The worker remains caught up in

> the hurly-burly of work-and-nothing-else, in the fine-spun exhausting game of sophistical phrase-mongering, into incessant "entertainment" by empty stimulants—in short, into a no-man's-land which may be quite comfortably furnished, but which has no place for the serenity of intrinsically meaningful activity, for contemplation, and certainly not for festivity.[7]

Retrieving overlooked aspects of our own Greek heritage plays a key role in Pieper's account of authenticity. In Plato's *Symposium*, for instance, Pieper focuses his attention on the character Apollodorus, who before meeting Socrates was ambitiously caught up in the bustle of the marketplace. "I went about," says Apollodorus, "driven along by events, and thought I was being very busy, while at the same time I was more wretched than anyone."[8] It was Socrates who introduced him to "leisure" (*skole*), a life that had been freed from workaday ambition and the need for mastery over beings.[9] The Greeks, according to Pieper, had a very different interpretation of busy-ness and work. These terms were interpreted only negatively. Indeed, the Greeks did not even have a word for work. Rather, "to work" is to be "un-leisurely."

> Literally, the Greek says "we are unleisurely in order to have leisure." "To be unleisurely"—that is the word the Greeks used not only for the daily toil and moil of life, but for the ordinary everyday work. Greek only has the negative, *a-scolia*, just as Latin has *neg-otium*.[10]

Pieper suggests that the Greeks would have been confused by our modern emphasis on busy-ness and work because, as Aristotle confirms in the *Politics*, leisure is to be understood as "the centre-point about which everything revolves."[11] For the Greeks, therefore, the contemporary motto, "one does not work to live; one lives to work," would be absurd. Aristotle reverses this dictum when he says, "The goal of [work] is leisure."[12]

From the modern perspective that privileges busy-ness and productivity, the Greek conception of leisure, according to Pieper, appears as "something wholly fortuitous and strange, without rhyme or reason, and, normally speaking, unseemly: another word for laziness, idleness and sloth."[13] On this view, hard work represents the cure to one of the seven cardinal sins, the despair of idleness and boredom—which Pieper traces back to the Greek term *acedia*. But leisure is nothing like idleness. Indeed, idleness is the utter absence of leisure.

> Idleness, in the old sense of the word, so far from being synonymous with leisure, is more nearly the inner prerequisite which renders leisure impossible: it might be described as the utter absence of leisure, or the very opposite of leisure. . . . Idleness and the incapacity for leisure correspond with one another. Leisure is the contrary of both.[14]

What Pieper is suggesting in this passage is that the modern emphasis on busy-ness *and* the despair of boredom amount to the same thing, a fundamental indifference to the most serious, unsettling questions of life. Pieper's views resonate strongly with Heidegger's position.

As we saw in chapter 5, Heidegger interprets boredom as the mood that reveals the underlying emptiness of modern life insofar as it has become wholly preoccupied with consuming and producing beings. It is on the basis of this utilitarian worldview that all beings become equalized. This makes it increasingly difficult to qualitatively distinguish which worldly choices and commitments matter to us, because beings show up in only one way, as objects to be used and manipulated. The consequence is a disposition of indifference to the world, to "beings as a whole." The world is boring, because we are "entranced" (*bannen*) by the technological frenzy of things and remain oblivious to the enigmatic movement of being and to the meaning of our own being. In this regard, boredom is particularly dangerous, because our very busy-ness conceals the oppressiveness of our own indifference. In short, the cultural atmosphere of boredom in the technological age is embodied in the fact that we are too busy, too restless to be bored, to experience our own emptiness. Thus "this absence of oppressiveness," as Heidegger says, "is only apparently hidden; it is rather attested by the very activities with which we busy ourselves in our contemporary restlessness" (FCM, 164).

For Pieper and Heidegger, therefore, the despair of *acedia* in the modern age stems not from idleness or sloth but comes from an inability to step outside of the accelerated busy-ness of the work world. In his *Contributions*, Heidegger refers to this inability as "not-being-able-to-bear-the-stillness" (CP, 84), and Pieper calls it the "incapacity for leisure."[15] The leisurely attitude, in this regard, has nothing to do with recreation or time off from work. Weekends and vacations are still largely interpreted through the lens of busy-ness. They are not only caught up in the familiar consumption of beings—shopping, dining, movies, travel—but they are also viewed instrumentally as a means to an end to the extent that they rest and refresh us for the sake of becoming more efficient and productive workers. Thus the modern holiday is, as Heidegger says, "essentially correlated to workdays, [it is] taken to be just an interruption in our working time . . . nothing more than a pause that is established, finally for the sake of work itself" (RE, 126). Pieper echoes this sentiment when he writes:

> A break in one's work, whether of an hour, a day, or a week, is still part of the world of work. It is a link in the chain of utilitarian functions. The pause is made for the sake of work and in order to work, and a man is not only refreshed *from* work but *for* work . . . the point of leisure is not to be a restorative, a pick-me-up, whether mental or physical. . . . That is not the point.[16]

Identifying a core theme that was already crucial to Heidegger's project, Pieper suggests that leisure might best be understood as a form of "play" (*Spiel*), a nonwillful activity that is meaningful in itself and has no rational purpose or measurable use.[17] Pieper rejects the commonly held view that play is to be interpreted as a form of relaxation, diversion, or entertainment—playing golf, racquetball, and video games—that is less significant, less serious, than the reality of hard work. Heidegger's student Eugen Fink is helpful in this regard when he suggests that play should be viewed as an essential structure or condition of existence, what Heidegger would call an "existentiale" (*Existenzial*). Fink writes:

> Play is not only a peripheral manifestation of human life; it is not a contingent phenomenon that emerges upon occasion.

In essence, it comes under the ontological dispositions of human existence. It is a fundamental phenomenon.[18]

Here play is regarded as "just as original and basic in itself as death, work, and domination."[19] Opposed to the rationally controlled atmosphere of work and busy-ness, purposeless play opens us up to the primordial "event" (*Ereignis*) of being, that "brings forth," "gathers," and "appropriates" beings, allowing them to emerge-into-presence as the very beings that they are. For Heidegger, being, understood as the appropriating event, is itself playful to the extent that it hides from us. [20] Being reveals itself in particular ways only in terms of the beings that show up or emerge within it. Thus we cannot point to or find the openness. The luminosity of being that allows beings to appear is self-concealing. Heidegger explains:

> If we stand in a clearing in the woods, we see only what can be found within it: the free place, the trees about—and precisely not the luminosity of the clearing itself. As little as the openness is simply the unconcealedness of beings, but is the clearing *for* the self-concealing, so little is this self-concealment a mere being-absent. It is rather a vacillating, hesitant refusal. (BQP, 178)

Play, in this regard, has a twofold meaning. First, play can be interpreted as a kind of spontaneous, leisurely activity that frees us from the stress of our workaday existence and opens us up to a horizon of disclosure that is mysterious and incalculable, "where man," as Fink writes, "experiences the proximity of the gods, heroes, the dead, and where he [finds] himself in the presence of all of the beneficent and dreadful powers of the universe."[21] Second, play can be interpreted as the abyssal ground of being itself, what Heidegger will call the original "play" (*Spiel*) of "time-space" (*Zeit-Raum*), the self-concealing clearing within which all beings manifest, emerging and withdrawing in different ways, in different historical epochs (CP, 263–64). Thus the activity of play, understood in the first sense, reveals our absorption into play but, understood in the second sense, an absorption into the primordial opening on the basis of which beings can come into play. In this regard, "all playing," as Gadamer says, "is a being-played."[22]

In his writings on Hölderlin, Heidegger situates this kind of playful activity in communal celebrations or festivals. Heidegger interprets the festival in terms of the holiday ("holy-day"), as an event that celebrates and remembers the sacred rituals, myths, and practices that root us to a particular dwelling place or "homeland" (*Heimat*), creating a sense of belonging to regions and communities with a shared history. These premodern festivals might include the seasonal celebrations that follow a bountiful harvest, the public performances of Sophocles' tragedies at the Greek amphitheatre, or the Christian Eucharist that gives thanks to divine mystery. Such events stand outside of the workaday horizon of willful mastery and self-certainty and reacquaint us with an affirmation of the unsettledness and fragility of the world, of beings *as a whole*.[23]

In his reading of Hölderlin's poem "As When On a Holiday . . . ," Heidegger develops this point by drawing our attention to the following lines that capture the source of the festive temperament:

> Above the gods of Occident and Orient
> Nature is now awakening with the clang of arms,
> And from high Aether down to the abyss,
> According to firm law, as once, begotton out of holy Chaos,
> Inspiration, the all-creative,
> Again feels herself anew. (OH, 68)

According to Heidegger, Hölderlin's use of the word "nature" (*Die Natur*) is not to be interpreted in modern terms—as material bodies in causal interaction or as a standing reserve of calculable resources to be manipulated and consumed—but in terms of the Greek word for nature, *physis*, understood as the enigmatic "movement" (*Bewegung*) of "emerging and arising, [of] self opening," whereby beings initially "blossom forth" out of concealment (QCT, 10). Nature, based on this view, is the primordial "lighting of that clearing (*Lichtung*) into which anything may enter appearing, present itself in its outline, show itself in its 'appearance' and be present *as this or that*" (OH, 79, emphasis added). The "holy" (*Heilig*), therefore, is the awesome chaos of nature itself that engulfs us, "the yawning, gaping chasm, the open that first opens itself, wherein everything is engulfed" (OH, 85). The celebration of our belongingness to nature transports us out of the "dull and gloom of everyday [busy-ness]" and gives birth to the primordial temperament of wonder and awe (RE, 126).

In his 1937–38 Freiburg lecture, "The Basic Questions of Philosophy: Selected 'Problems' of 'Logic,'" Heidegger offers his most sustained analysis of wonder. For Heidegger, wonder is not to be confused with marveling at the unfamiliar, at "exceptional, unexpected, surprising" things. Marveling at the latest technological construct—the newest car, the biggest casino, the latest Hollywood blockbuster—is nothing more than curiosity. Here, the routine production of the uncommon that "bewitches and encharms" us becomes permanent, a commonplace (BQP, 136). Heidegger explains using the example of the movie industry.

> The uncommon thus obtains its own permanent character, form, and fashion. To do so it even requires an insidious habituality. We might think in passing of all the extraordinary things the cinema must offer continually; what is new every day and never happened before becomes something habitual and always the same. (BQP, 137)

The original disposition of wonder is distinct from everyday forms of marveling at what is newest and latest to the extent that it is not restricted to individual beings—cars, casinos, movies—that are taken as unusual. Rather, in wonder, the world *as a whole* shows up as unusual, "anything whatsoever as such and *everything as everything* become the most unusual" (BQP, 144). In this sense, wonder is not a curious distraction or diversion from the usual. In wonder, there is "no escape" from the unusual, no rational explanation that can penetrate it. In this regard, Heidegger will refer to wonder as being "in between" the usual and the unusual, because one does "not know the way out or the way in" (BQP, 145).

In a state of wonder, the authentic self does not panic, "does not desire help," but rather opens himself or herself up to and occupies the wondrous "between," the abyssal, free openness where beings *as a whole* come into play. Heidegger says:

> Wonder now opens up what alone is wondrous in it: namely, the whole as the whole, the whole as beings, beings as a whole, that they are and what they are, beings as beings. What is meant here by the "as" is the "between" that wonder separates out, the open of a free space hardly surmised and heeded, in which beings *come into play as such*, namely, as the beings they are, *in the play of their being.* (BQP, 146, emphases added)

Heidegger is suggesting that wonder does not separate us from the commonplace. Indeed, "wonder sets *us* before the usual itself, precisely as what is the most unusual" (BQP, 150). In short, the most ordinary claim that *"beings are"* is now experienced as wondrous. Wonder is the mood that "displaces us before and into the unusualness of everything in its usualness" (BQP, 150). Leisure, in this regard, is an active embodiment of wonder over the fact that "there is something rather than nothing, that there are beings and we ourselves are in their midst."[24] Needless to say, this ancient disposition has been forgotten in the age of modern busy-ness. Today, the claim "beings are" is, according to Heidegger, not even worth questioning; it is interpreted as redundant, as "obvious, empty talk" (BQP, 168).

The displacement of wonder is accompanied by shock or "startled dismay" (*Erschrecken*), because the self of everydayness—who understands everything—is thrown into a state of deep questioning, into the mystery that "beings are." Heidegger will refer to this as a kind of "suffering" (*Leiden*), but a suffering that is not to be interpreted in the common "Christian-moralistic-psychological way," as a submission to life's woes. Rather, the suffering of wonder refers to a radical acceptance or tolerance for mystery, a "letting oneself be transformed" by the enigmatic openness of being that appropriates and gathers beings (BQP, 151). Thus authentic suffering comes from a "genuine" (*eigentlich*) willingness to let beings be, to dwell in the questionability of beings, which enables one to "draw close to [the] openness, without falling prey to the temptation to explain it prematurely" (BQP, 178). This conception of authenticity that emerges in the late 1930s bears a striking resemblance to how authenticity was originally conceived in his early Freiburg lectures. In his 1921–22 lectures on Aristotle, for instance, Heidegger identifies the struggle for "questionability" as *the* key characteristic of authenticity, a characteristic that can keep us close to truth—understood as the original emerging-forth of beings out of concealment—by resisting the already understood assumptions and prejudices of our own "factical" (*faktisch*) situation. Questioning involves coming to grips with our own history in order to "let what is coming occur" on its own terms (PIA, 112, 114). Based on this view, questioning is not a sign of weakness or insecurity. It is the steadfast awareness that everything is not obvious and explainable by rational principles (BQP, 169).

The interpretation of authenticity that I am offering suggests that the historical retrieval of leisure may provide contemporary Dasein with the means to be ready for the unsettling aspects of life, opening us up to a composed, patient disposition in the face of technological busy-ness, a disposition that "lets beings be." According to Heidegger, the origins of our current technological worldview are to be found in ancient Greece. In this epoch, technology did not manifest itself in terms of forceful mastery and manipulation but was experienced as something poetic, embodied in the craftsman or artisan who employed *technē* in order to "bring forth" and "preserve" the wondrous, allowing things to "thing," to emerge-into-presence as they are given naturally, independently of humans (QCT, 13; BQP, 154). Because the Greeks were attuned—by the temperament of wonder—to the sacred emerging forth of beings, they exhibited a reverence and harmony with nature, letting beings come forth on their own terms.

However, for Heidegger, authenticity, understood in terms of the complete retrieval and repetition of the original Greek temperament, is impossible. Repetition is always incomplete to the extent that a hermeneutic situation—a pregiven cultural background of assumptions, institutions, and practices—always colors any recovery. "What has-been-there" can be handed down to us, therefore, only in terms of today's situation, namely, the harried world of planetary technology.[25] The question we are left with is this: Can an authentic retrieval of leisure take place today, in an age when the gods have fled, when the ancient sense of festivity has been obliterated, when technological progress, production, and busy-ness appear to be the only game in town?

Heidegger may offer reason for hope in his 1953 lecture "The Question Concerning Technology" when he writes this:

> We are thereupon summoned to hope in the growing light of the saving power. How can this happen? *Here and now and in little things*, that we may foster the saving power in its increase. This includes always holding before our eyes the extreme danger.[26] (QCT, 33, emphasis added)

This passage indicates that we are, undeniably, in danger to the extent that modern technology dominates our everyday lives and enframes the totality of beings. But it also appears to suggest that *das Man* is far too complex to be captured in one, monological worldview. The world is also composed of "little things," of smaller communities and practices that remain on the margins of mainstream busy-ness and productivity and constitute an overlooked fringe of our hermeneutic situation. These marginal practices may provide modern culture with a connective thread back to the ancient temperament by celebrating our fragile belongingness to the movement of being. These communal or solitary acts of resistance are embodied in leisure and might include walking slowly in the nearby woods, playing music with friends, sitting quietly by a lake, looking deeply into a lover's eyes, or perhaps even focusing on one's breath when stuck in traffic, just to be in the wondrous midst of beings, to be near the trees, the lake, the body that breathes.[27] Nietzsche beautifully captures this kind of purposeless, nonattached play in his poem "Sils Maria":

> Here I sat waiting, waiting—yet for nothing,
> beyond good and evil, sometimes enjoying light,
> sometimes enjoying shadow, completely only play,
> completely lake, completely noon,
> completely time without goal.[28]

Heidegger makes it clear that authentic action will not save us from planetary technology. Genuine leisure, in this regard, is simply an act of readiness, of being prepared for the culmination of the technological age, a culmination that is marked when all beings are forced to show up in only one way, when every mystery and every god has been forgotten. Leisure and festivity can only keep us in contact with wonder, with other, more original horizons, and, perhaps, steady us for the possibility of the emergence of the "other beginning," one that does not master and control beings but rather lets beings be. Heidegger makes no guarantees but wants us to be prepared "so that we do not, simply put, die meaningless deaths, but that when we decline, we decline in the face of the absent god."[29]

There is, however, something fundamentally unsatisfying with this interpretation of authenticity insofar as it represents a kind of passive resignation to the threat of modern technology, a threat of such urgency that the very survival of humankind and the planet as a whole is at stake. Heidegger, in this regard, often appears fatalistic by suggesting that there is no human way to overcome the danger of "enframing" (*Gestell*). It is our inevitable fate, a "destining" (*Geschick*) of the eschatological movement of Western "history" (*Geschichte*) itself (QCT, 24). It is for this reason that Heidegger claims enframing "will never allow itself to be mastered either positively or negatively by a human doing" (TU, 38). This means "human activity can never . . . counter the danger" and "human achievement . . . can never banish it" (QCT, 33). This position has led a number of critics to accuse Heidegger of rendering us powerless concerning the global threat of *Gestell*.[30] Julian Young sums up the problem this way:

> [D]o not [Heidegger's] reflections still reduce us to impotent spectators, the victims rather than makers of history? Is it not indeed the case that they render "every attempt to

build from the ruins of our culture a house in which we
can dwell" utterly futile?[31]

With this fatalistic reading, it appears that all we can do is wait
patiently and quietly for history to send us a new horizon of disclosure that may grant us the power to save the earth and ourselves.
Thus Heidegger claims that "man['s] . . . essence is to be the one who
waits" (TU, 42). But waiting does not mean that human beings are
impotent in addressing the danger. Heidegger writes:

> Does this mean that man, for better or worse, is helplessly
> delivered over to technology? No, it means the direct oppo-
> site; and not only that, but essentially it means something
> more than the opposite, because it means something dif-
> ferent. (TU, 37)

Waiting is not a disposition of helpless resignation; it is an active
attempt to disengage from the everyday modes of calculative busy-ness
itself. By "dwelling" in a nonwillful, playful way, we can begin to free
ourselves from the narrow, manipulative horizon of planetary technology and enter into, what Heidegger calls, the "open region," a horizon
of disclosure that does not master and control beings but, rather, lets
beings be (ET, 125). Indeed, it is this act of freeing, releasing, or letting
go of things that Heidegger will refer to as the "saving power."

> What does "to save" mean? It means to loose, to emancipate,
> to free, to spare and husband, to harbor protectingly, to take
> under one's care, to keep safe . . . to put something back into
> what is proper and right, into the essential. (TU, 42)

It is here that we can bring to a close our discussion of the body by
exploring what Heidegger means by dwelling understood as a way
of being-in-the-world that frees and preserves things by letting them
be and gesturing toward aspects of embodiment that can open us up
to this way of being.

Conclusion

Embodied Dwelling

In his 1942–43 essay, "On the Essence of Truth," Heidegger explains that freeing beings or "letting beings be" (*Gelassenheit*) is not to be interpreted negatively in the sense of renouncing, neglecting, or being indifferent to beings. It is "rather the opposite. To let be is to engage oneself with beings" (ET, 125). This freeing engagement no longer forces beings into the totalizing framework of modern technology. Instead, it lets beings be as the mysterious beings that they are. Here Heidegger is offering an alternative to the traditional definition of human freedom, where freedom (conceived negatively) is the absence of constraint with respect to what we can or cannot do or (conceived positively) the ability to choose one course of action over another. For Heidegger, there is a more primordial sense of freedom that refers to our engagement with the "openness of the open region," the "there" ("*Da*") that frees beings (ET, 126). The act of freeing beings also frees us by simplifying our lives, releasing us from our own obsessions with calculative mastery and control, allowing us to experience the simple, uncanny "free-play" where beings are preserved by being allowed to emerge-into-presence on their own terms. In his *Contributions*, Heidegger explains:

> One must be equipped for the inexhaustibility of the simple so that it no longer withdraws from him . . . [but can] be found again in each being. . . . But we attain the simple only by preserving each thing, each being—in the free-play of its mystery, and do not believe that we seize be-ing by analyzing our already-firm knowledge of a thing's properties. (CP, 196)

Here we need to get a clearer sense of the thing that is preserved by the act of freeing. We need to ask the obvious question: "What is a thing?" (TT, 164)

143

Before beginning this investigation, we have to recall that for the Heidegger of *Being and Time* things come into being only against the unfolding background of a world, understood as an interconnected nexus of sociohistorical relations. In his later writings, this notion of world is expanded to include not only the shared equipment, myths, institutions, and discursive practices of Dasein but also plants and animals, bodies of water, geological formations, the movement of the seasons, and the cosmos as a whole. The world is now interpreted in terms of what Heidegger calls "the fourfold" (*das Geviert*), including the interconnected elements of "earth," "sky," "divinities," and "mortals." In his 1951 lecture, "Building Dwelling Thinking," Heidegger explains the characteristics of the fourfold that, taken together, constitute a "simple oneness."

> Earth is the serving bearer, blossoming and fruiting, spreading out in rock and water, rising up into plant and animal. . . . Sky is the vaulting path of the sun, the course of the changing moon, the wandering glitter of the stars, the year's seasons and their changes, the light and dusk of day, the gloom and glow of night, the clemency and inclemency of the weather, the drifting clouds and blue depth of the ether. . . . The divinities are the beckoning messengers of the godhead. Out of the holy sway of the godhead, the god appears in his presence or withdraws into his concealment. . . . The mortals are the human beings. They are called mortals because they can die. To die means to be capable of death as death. Only man dies, and indeed continually, as long as he remains on earth, under the sky, before divinities. (BDT, 351–352)

The fourfold is the dynamic, interdependent web of relations on the basis of which a thing can be the kind of thing that it is. A thing, in this regard, is not a static entity with useful properties that can be manipulated for certain purposes. Rather, the thing is the event or happening of, what Heidegger calls, "thinging." Thinging is the "gathering" together of the world. Each thing—a bridge, a jug, a river, a mountain—gathers the interconnected elements of the fourfold together. Thus *"thing* means gathering" (TT, 172, emphasis added). Zen poet Thich Nhat Hanh provides a perfect example of Heidegger's sense of gathering with his description of a particular thing, in this case, a sheet of paper:

If you are a poet, you will see clearly that there is a cloud floating in this sheet of paper. Without a cloud, there will be no rain; without rain, the trees cannot grow, and without trees we cannot make paper. The cloud is essential for the paper to exist. If the cloud is not here, the sheet of paper cannot be here either. . . .

If we look into this sheet of paper even more deeply, we can see the sunshine in it. If the sunshine is not there, the tree cannot grow. In fact, nothing can grow. Even we cannot grow without sunshine. And so, we know that the sunshine is also in this sheet of paper. The paper and the sunshine inter-are. And if we continue to look, we see the logger who cut the tree and brought it to the mill to be transformed into paper. And we see the wheat. We know that the logger cannot exist without his daily bread, and therefore the wheat that became his bread is also in this sheet of paper. And the logger's father and mother are there too. . . .

You cannot point out one thing that is not here—time, space, the earth, the rain, the minerals in the soil, the sunshine, the cloud, the river, the heat. Everything co-exists with this sheet of paper. . . . As thin as this sheet of paper is, it contains everything in the universe.[32]

Thich Nhat Hanh is showing how a thing is always mutually interdependent on all other things, and that there are no enduring, self-existing entities. Each thing, says Heidegger, is in a state of "mirror-play" with all of the elements of the world. Each thing "dances," playfully emerging and withdrawing in the "ring" of the fourfold's movement.

The mirror-play of world is the round dance of [appropriation]. . . . The round dance is the ring that joins while it plays as mirroring. . . . Out of the ringing mirror-play the thinging of the thing takes place. (TT, 177–178)

This means that I—as an *ek-static*, bodily thing—am not bounded and isolated by my skin. In my everyday activities, I stretch into the world, mirror the world, and gather the natural and cultural elements of the fourfold together. "I am never here only as this encapsulated body," says Heidegger; "rather, I am *there*, that is, I already pervade [the world] and thus can go through it" (BDT, 359, emphasis added). Consequently, from the perspective of the fourfold, it is impossible to

tell where my body ends and the world begins, because I *am* a site
of the dynamic interplay that makes up the world. Yet it is important
not to mistake my body as simply the combination or unity of the
various elements of the fourfold. Gail Stenstad correctly points out
that in the gathering together of the fourfold, each thing reveals itself
as "something dif-ferent, something carried apart" from every other
thing. To the extent that each thing is enjoined to the fourfold in a
particular way, from a particular time and place, each thing is always
unique, an "ever- changing web of fluid and complex relations."[33]

By freeing things or letting things be, Heidegger is calling for
humans (mortals) to preserve and "care-for" the mysterious and
fragile interconnectedness of things, because this interconnectedness
is nothing less than the world itself. "The simple onefold of sky and
earth, mortals and divinities . . . [that] we call the world" (TT, 179).
To dwell, in this regard, is to "care-for each thing in its own nature."
Heidegger writes the following:

> To free really means to care-for [*schonen*]. The caring-for
> itself consists not only in the fact that we do no harm to
> that which is cared-for. Real caring-for is something posi-
> tive and happens when . . . we gather something back into
> its nature, when we "free" it in the real sense of the word
> into a preserve of peace. To dwell, to be set at peace, means
> to remain at peace within the free sphere that cares-for
> each thing in its own nature. The fundamental character
> of dwelling is this caring-for.[34] (BDT, 351)

Dwelling, therefore, requires preserving or caring-for the elements
of the fourfold that make up the world. First, "mortals dwell in that
they save the earth" by letting the earth be and freeing it from the
instrumental subjugation and exploitation of *Gestell*. Second, "mortals
dwell in that they receive the sky as sky" by recognizing the way
that we belong to the rhythms of the seasons, climate, weather, and
the cosmos as a whole. Third, "mortals dwell in that they await the
divinities as divinities" by understanding cultural gods in terms of
the shared ethos of a particular historical community and not hypos-
tasizing gods as idols that are universal and timeless. Fourth, "mortals
dwell in that they initiate their own [capacity] for death as death"
by acknowledging the fundamental finitude and impermanence of
the human condition (BDT, 352). However, because each element in
the fourfold is relationally bound into a onefold, the four modes of

dwelling-as-preserving can be reduced to one mode, where dwelling is simply being "near" or "staying with" things (BDT, 353).

Dwelling, in this sense, is to stay with/near the things that make up a particular living "space" (*Raum*). As we saw earlier, space is not a reference to a geometrical coordinate system within which objects are located. It is, rather, a place where the "mirror-play" of natural and cultural features comes together, and we experience this web of relations in terms of familiarity and belongingness. In describing what constitutes staying with/near things in a particular living space, Heidegger identifies a twofold path. He writes: "Mortals [1] nurse and nurture the things that grow and [2] specially construct things that do not" (BDT, 353). The first path relates to how mortals let go of natural things—the mountain, the river, the forest—so that these things can grow, emerge, or be "brought forth" on their own. The gardener, for instance, cares-for plants by letting go of them, allowing for "the bursting of the blossom into bloom, in itself" (QCT, 10). The second path relates to how things are brought forth on the basis of human building and construction in a way that is in harmony or rapport with nature. Instead of regarding nature as a standing reserve independent of us to be exploited by modern technology, dwelling requires an attentiveness to and reverence for our interconnectedness to a particular region or space of concern.

The craftsman who works with wood, for instance, is aware of the dynamic nexus of relations that make up her or his living space. She or he is respectful of the kinds of trees—birch, pine, evergreen—that grow on the local hillside and how the stream coming down from the mountain nourishes the trees, and how the winter snows high on the mountain feed the stream in the spring. The craftsman, in this regard, is aware that the whole of the craft is dependent on a fragile web of relations that gathers together a particular living space, and this web limits how man-made things can be brought forth out of the wood. Heidegger offers an example with the following description of a cabinetmaker.

> [The cabinetmaker's] learning is not mere practice, to gain facility in the use of tools. Nor does he merely gather knowledge about the customary forms of the things he is to build. If he is to become a true cabinetmaker, he makes himself answer and respond above all to the different kinds of wood and to the shapes slumbering within wood—to wood as it enters into man's dwelling with all the hidden

riches of its essence. In fact, this relatedness to wood is
what maintains the whole craft. Without that relatedness,
the craft will never be anything but empty busywork, any
occupation with it will be determined exclusively by business concerns. (WCT, 14–15)

The cabinetmaker does not view the forest instrumentally, as a stockpile
of wood to be exploited for cabinetmaking. She or he understands
the forest in terms of its binding relationship to a home, to a site of
gathering nearness.

At the beginning of his 1951 essay "The Thing," Heidegger
explains why staying with things or being in "the nearness" (*die Nähe*)
is so difficult in the age of *Gestell*, because we no longer belong to
a particular living space. For Heidegger, this sense of belongingness
to a shared place—to a homeland with unique practices, myths,
geography, and climate—is being destroyed by modern technology,
by jet travel, cell phones, television, radio, and the Internet. We are,
today, everywhere and nowhere all at once. We no longer experience nearness (or remoteness) to things, because distance itself has
been obliterated.

What is nearness if it fails to come about despite the reduc-
tion of the longest distances to the shortest intervals? What is
nearness if it is repelled by the abolition of distances? What
is nearness if, along with its failure to appear, remoteness
also remains absent.... Everything gets lumped together
in a uniform distancelessness. How? Is not this merging
of everything into the distanceless more unearthly than
everything bursting apart? (TT, 163–164)

To the extent that *Gestell* abolishes distance and uproots us from nearness, we are unable to stay with things, which suggests that we are
unable "[to] spare and protect the thing's presence in the region from
which it presences" (TT, 179).

For Heidegger, to dwell in nearness requires us to question the
monolithic worldview of modern technology and the disembodied,
calculative way of being that comes with it, because it is this way
of being that uproots us from what is near. "In order to experience
this face-to-face [with] things [in the world]," says Heidegger, "we
must...first rid ourselves of the calculative frame of mind" (NL,
104; FS, 71). Dwelling, therefore, demands a letting go of dualistic,
re-presentational thinking, where the encapsulated subject or "I" is set

over and against a world of objects. To be near things is to *embody* dwelling in such a way that we encounter things intimately in their/ our contiguous, gathering entwinement. It is only in the proximity of bodily presence—in smelling, hearing, seeing, touching—that we can experience things thinging as they emerge and come forth, gathering together the elements of the fourfold. Here the body is not regarded as it is in the Platonic-Cartesian tradition, as an epistemological obstacle to our access to clear and distinct knowledge, access that can only be granted to a detached *ego cogito*. Indeed, from the perspective of embodied dwelling, there is no separation of mind and body or of body and world. Heidegger is correct when he says that this shift in orientation is "so simple that it is extremely difficult to explain philosophically" (FS, 72).

In opening myself to the dynamic interplay of the fourfold, my body and world merge together in, what Heidegger calls, "the disposition of the heart," an embodied disposition that gathers together my personal memories and goals for the future; it gathers the shared ethos of my historical community and the discursive practices that I grow into; it gathers the genetic, skeletal, and hormonal signature that makes me the corporeal being that I am; it gathers the geography of my particular homeland, my proximity to the sun, the mountains, and the ocean (WCT, 140). In his 1951–52 lecture, "What Is Called Thinking?," Heidegger refers to embodied thinking that is tuned to our interdependence with the fourfold in terms of the "thanc." Going back to the Old English, Heidegger finds a point of convergence between the words *thencan* ("to think) and *thancian* ("to thank") (WCT, 139). For Heidegger, "original thanking is the thanks owed for being" (WCT, 141). It is a way of thinking that expresses awe and gratitude for the fragile gathering together of the elements that allow the thinging of things, allowing me to be the ek-static bodily being that I am, on this earth, under this sky, among these divinities, as I move toward my own death. Heidegger says it all when he writes this:

> The *thanc*, the heart's core, is the gathering of all that concerns us, all that we care for, all that touches us insofar as we are, as human beings. . . . In a certain manner, we ourselves are that gathering. (WCT, 144)

To the extent that our lives are enframed by an accelerated, calculative horizon that seeks to control and master beings, we have forgotten how to think in terms of this primordial experience of awe and gratitude, of being tuned to the mysterious openness that lets beings be.

Does this mean that Heidegger is a radical antimodernist or Luddite who is urging us to abandon the faceless urban centers where technology thrives? This familiar reading is certainly reinforced by Heidegger's own biography, "his taste for peasant costume, the hut in the Black Forest, the refusal of the chair in Berlin, and so on."[35] Without question, the frenzied, instrumental life of the modern metropolis has a tendency to cover over the possibility for authentic dwelling and our capacity to be near things and give thanks to our interdependence on the fourfold. Yet Heidegger is not simply waxing nostalgic and longing for the simple, premodern life of the Bavarian peasant. He makes it clear that technology does not need to be overcome or abandoned altogether in order to dwell in embodied thankfulness. The aim of Heidegger's project is to question the technological way of being and acknowledge that calculative disclosure is only one of countless ways that beings can be revealed. Dwelling, therefore, does not regard technology as something "devil[ish]," something that needs to be "attacked blindly." Dwelling simply demands letting go of the totalizing horizon of technology itself so that we "do not cling one-sidedly to a single idea" (DT, 55). In remaining open to the mystery of the "play of time-space," we can still affirm the use of technology, but we do not need to be enslaved by it as the *only possible* worldview. In his 1955 Memorial Address in Messkirch, Heidegger explains:

> We can use technical devices and yet with proper use also keep ourselves so free of them, that we may let go of them any time. We can use technical devices as they ought to be used, and also let them alone as something which does not affect our inner and real core. We can affirm the unavoidable use of technical devices, and also deny them the right to dominate us, and so to warp, confuse, and lay waste to our nature. (DT, 54)

It is in releasing ourselves from the dazzling, reifying grip of modern technology and opening up to our own belongingness to the ever-changing, relational interplay of things that we can begin to dwell in the world in a totally different way. For Heidegger, this kind of embodied dwelling "promise[s] us a new ground and foundation upon which we can stand and endure in the world of technology without being imperiled by it" (DT, 55).

Notes

Introduction

1. Alphonse de Waelhens, "The Philosophy of the Ambiguous," in *The Structure of Behavior,* by Maurice Merleau-Ponty, trans. Alden L. Fisher (Boston, MA: Beacon Press, 1963), xix.

2. See Richard Askay's "Heidegger, the Body, and the French Philosophers," *Continental Philosophy Review* 32 (1999): 29–35.

3. See Hubert Dreyfus, *Being-in-the-World: A Commentary on Heidegger's* Being and Time, *Division I* (Cambridge, MA: MIT Press, 1991); David Cerbone, "Heidegger and Dasein's Bodily Nature: What Is the Hidden Problematic?," *International Journal of Philosophical Studies* 33 (2000): 209–230; David Krell, *Daimon Life: Heidegger and Life-Philosophy* (Bloomington: Indiana University Press, 1992).

4. Krell, *Daimon Life,* 152.

5. Michel Haar asks, "[C]an one phenomenologically and ontologically justify placing the body in a secondary position in the existential analytic? [In Heidegger], there are barely a few allusions without really explicit references to the hand that handles tools." See *The Song of the Earth: Heidegger and the Grounds of the History of Being,* trans. Reginald Lilly (Bloomington: Indiana University Press, 1993), 34.

6. See Jacques Derrida, *Of Spirit: Heidegger and the Question,* trans. Geoffrey Bennington and Rachel Bowlby (Chicago, IL: University of Chicago Press, 1989); Derrida, "*Geschlecht* II: Heidegger's Hand," in *Deconstruction and Philosophy: The Texts of Jacques Derrida,* ed. John Sallis, 161–96 (Chicago, IL: University of Chicago Press, 1987); Didier Franck, "Being and the Living," in *Who Comes after the Subject?,* ed. Eduardo Cadava, Peter Connor, and Jean-Luc Nancy, 135–47 (New York: Routledge, 1991); Jean-Luc Nancy, *The Sense of the World,* trans. Jeffrey S. Librett (Minneapolis: University of Minnesota Press, 1997); Michel Haar, *The Song of the Earth: Heidegger and the Grounds of the History of Being,* trans. Reginald Lilly (Bloomington: Indiana University Press, 1993); Giorgio Agamben, *The Open: Man and Animal* (Stanford, CA: Stanford University Press, 2004); William McNeill, "Life beyond the Organism: Animal Being in Heidegger's Freiburg Lectures, 1929–30," in *Animal Others: On Ethics, Ontology, and Animal Life,* ed. H. Peter Steeves, 197–248 (Albany: State University of New York Press, 1999); Krell, *Daimon Life;* Simon Glendinning,

"Heidegger and the Question of Animality," *International Journal of Philosophic Studies* 4:1 (1996): 67–86; David Cerbone, "Heidegger and Dasein's Bodily Nature: What Is the Hidden Problematic?," *International Journal of Philosophic Studies* 8:2 (2000): 209–30; Matthew Calarco, "Heidegger's Zoontology," in *Animal Philosophy: Essential Readings in Continental Thought*, ed. Matthew Calarco and Peter Atterton, 18–30 (New York: Continuum Press, 2005); Stuart Elden, "Heidegger's Animals," *Continental Philosophy Review* 39:3 (2006): 273–91; Frank Schalow, *The Incarnality of Being: The Earth, Animals, and the Body in Heidegger's Thought* (Albany: State University of New York Press, 2006).

    7. Cerbone, "Heidegger and Dasein's Bodily Nature," 210.

Chapter 1

    1. This colloquial translation of *"Wie steht es um das Sein?"* is taken from Charles Guignon in his essay "Being as Appearing: Retrieving the Greek Experience of *Physis*," in *A Companion to Heidegger's Introduction to Metaphysics*, ed. Richard Polt and Gregory Fried, 34 (New Haven, CT: Yale University Press, 2001).

    2. Jacques Derrida, *Writing and Difference*, trans. Alan Bass (Chicago, IL: University of Chicago Press, 1978), 279.

    3. Dorothea Frede, "The Question of Being: Heidegger's Project," in *The Cambridge Companion to Heidegger*, 2d ed., ed. Charles Guignon, 46 (New York: Cambridge University Press, 1993).

    4. In reference to Descartes, for instance, Heidegger writes:

> Whenever Descartes asks about the being of the entity he is asking, in the spirit of the tradition about *substance*. . . . Descartes here follows, not only in expression and concept but also in subject matter, the Scholastic and so basically the Greek formulation of the question of entities. . . . By substance we can understand nothing other than something which "is" in such a way that it needs no other entity in order to be. (HCT, 172)

    5. Max Weber, "Science as a Vocation," in *Max Weber, Essays in Sociology*, trans. H. Gerth and C. Wright Mills, 139 (New York: Oxford University Press, 1958).

    6. Ibid., 138, 143, 148.

    7. Ibid., 139–40.

    8. Heidegger, "On the Way Back into the Ground of Metaphysics," in *Existentialism from Dostoevsky to Sartre*, trans. and ed. Walter Kaufmann, 205 (New York: Meridian Books, 1956).

    9. This account is from a letter to Karl Löwith, dated August 19, 1921, in Löwith's *Aufsätze und Vorträge* (Stutgart: W. Kohlhammer, 1971), cited in Charles Guignon, *Heidegger and the Problem of Knowledge* (Indianapolis, IN: Hackett Press, 1983), 69.

10. Dreyfus, *Being-in-the-World*, 14–16, 24–26.

11. However, to say I "have" an understanding of being is misleading. I do not "have" an understanding as if it were a cognitive property or some piece of knowledge that I possess. Rather, as Heidegger writes, "[Dasein] *is* in such a way as to be its *there*. . . . [It] is cleared (*gelichtet*) in itself, not through any other entity, *but in such a way that it is itself the clearing*" (BT, 171, emphases added).

12. I am not born with this understanding. Rather, I "grow into" an understanding of being through a process of socialization. The biological fact of my bodily birth and genetic code is irrelevant; rather, it is *where* and especially *when* I am born that is important, because my current nexus of social relations will determine not only the way beings show up *as such* but also limit the possibilities (public roles, careers, paths, and relationships) that I can actively press into in the future.

13. This distinction between *Körper* and *Leib* is carefully spelled out in parts one and three, sections 28 and 62, of Husserl's 1936 work *The Crisis of European Sciences and Transcendental Philosophy*, trans. David Carr (Evanston, IL: Northwestern University Press, 1970).

14. See Guignon, *Heidegger and the Problem of Knowledge*, 61; Dreyfus, *Being-in-the-World*, 239.

15. I am indebted to Guignon for this account. See also Dreyfus, *Being-in-the-World*, 20.

16. Heidegger, "Phenomenology and Theology," in *Pathmarks*, trans. James G. Hart and John C. Maraldo, ed. William McNeill, 41 (New York: Cambridge University Press, 1998).

17. These examples are taken from Iain Thomson's article "Heidegger and the Politics of the University," *Journal of the History of Philosophy* 41:4 (2003): 528–29.

18. According to Heidegger, these a priori structures or conditions are already presupposed by the ontic sciences and their regional ontologies.

> The question of being aims therefore at ascertaining the a priori conditions not only for the possibility of the sciences, which examine entities as entities of such and such a type, and, in so doing, already operate with an understanding of being, but also for the possibility of those ontologies themselves, which are prior to the ontical sciences and which provide their foundations. (BT, 31)

19. For further reading concerning the problem of interpreting Heidegger as an existentialist, see Robert Scharff, "On 'Existentialist' Readings of Heidegger," *The Southwestern Journal of Philosophy* 1:2 (1978): 7–20; Kevin Aho, "Why Heidegger Is not an Existentialist: Interpreting Authenticity and Historicity in Being and Time," *Florida Philosophical Review* 3:2 (2003): 5–22.

20. Jean-Paul Sartre, "The Humanism of Existentialism," in *Existentialism: Basic Writings*, trans. Bernard Frechtman, ed. Charles Guignon and Derk Pereboom, 66–67 (Indianapolis, IN: Hackett Press, 2001).

21. Because of his association with existential phenomenology, Heidegger continually had to clarify and defend the distinction between Dasein and the concrete subject long after the publication *Being and Time*. In 1943, he writes:

> But how could this . . . become an explicit question before every attempt had been made to liberate the determination of human nature from the concept of subjectivity. . . . To characterize with a single term both the involvement of human being in human nature and the essential relation of man to the openness ("there") of being as such, the name of "being there [Dasein]" was chosen. . . . Any attempt, therefore, to rethink *Being and Time* is thwarted as long as one is satisfied with the observation that, in this study, the term "being there" is used in place of consciousness.

See Heidegger, "On the Way Back into the Ground of Metaphysics," 270, 271.

22. Hence, Dasein should not be translated literally, as "human existence" or "being-there." The emphasis is on *the* "there" as a disclosive region or space.

23. See Lawrence Hatab's discussion of "formal indication" in *Ethics and Finitude: Heideggerian Contributions to Moral Philosophy* (Lanham, MD: Rowman and Littlefield, 2000), 12–13.

24. It is for this reason that Heidegger says "every interpretation is never a *presuppositionless* apprehending of something presented to us" (BT, 191–92, emphasis added).

25. This may provide us with a clearer picture of Heidegger's claim in the Zollikon seminars, that "bodying-forth" (*leiben*) should be regarded as a "necessary" condition for any instance of Dasein, because it is an essential aspect of the temporal structure of situatedness (ZS, 197).

26. However, the body is not a sufficient condition, because it is nowhere to be found in the temporal structure of projection. Heidegger says: "Bodying forth (*leiben*) as such belongs to being-in-the-world. But being-in-the-world is not exhausted in bodying forth. For instance, the understanding [projection] of being also belongs to being-in-the-world" (ZS, 196).

Chapter 2

1. Richard Askay, who co-translated the Zollikon seminars, recognizes important points of convergence between Heidegger and Merleau-Ponty. He writes:

> Heidegger's lack of reference is all the more interesting given that Merleau-Ponty's account of the body came the closest (among the

French existentialist phenomenologists) to his own descriptions in the *Zollikon Seminars*. Some of their similarities included: their analysis of bodily being viz. (a) gesture and expression (b) bodily being and spatiality (c) refusing to see the body as merely a corporeal, self-contained object and (d) the phantom limb analysis.

See Askay, "Heidegger, the Body, and the French Philosophers," 29–35, esp. 31.

2. See Guignon, *Heidegger and the Problem of Knowledge*, 86, 104.

3. Pierre Bourdieu, *Outline of a Theory of Practice* (New York: Cambridge University Press, 1977), 87.

4. Dreyfus, *Being-in-the-World*, 137; Chanter, "The Problematic Normative Assumptions of Heidegger's Ontology," in *Feminist Interpretations of Martin Heidegger*, ed. Nancy Holland and Patricia Huntington, 80 (University Park: Pennsylvania State University Press, 2001).

5. Alphonse de Waelhens, "The Philosophy of the Ambiguous," xviii–xix.

6. See Dreyfus, *Being-in-the-World*, 137.

7. Sartre writes, "Heidegger does not make the slightest allusion to [the body] in his existential analytic with the result that his Dasein appears to us as asexual." Of course, as we will see in chapter 3, "asexuality" is precisely the way Heidegger would characterize Dasein. Dasein does not refer to the embodiments of "man" or "woman" with specific biological attributes. Dasein is already "there" prior to the determinate characteristics of beings like "man" or "woman" and should therefore be interpreted as "neutral," as "neither of the two sexes" (MFL, 136–37). See Jean-Paul Sartre, *Being and Nothingness*, trans. Hazel. E. Barnes (New York: Washington Square Press, 1956), 498.

8. Iris Marion Young, *Throwing Like a Girl and Other Essays in Feminist Philosophy and Social Theory* (Bloomington: Indiana University Press, 1990), 154.

9. Bourdieu describes how these workaday bodily movements already imply social domination and submission.

> Male, upward movements and female, downward movements, uprightness versus bending, the will to be on top, to overcome, versus submission—the fundamental oppositions of the social order—are always sexually over-determined, as if the body language of sexual domination and submission had provided the fundamental principles of both the body language and the verbal language of social domination and submission.

See Bourdieu, *The Logic of Practice*, trans. Richard Nice (Stanford, CA: Stanford University Press, 1990), 72.

10. Ibid., 70.

11. Young, *Throwing Like a Girl*, 155.

12. Monica Langer, *Merleau-Ponty's Phenomenology of Perception: A Guide and Commentary* (Tallahassee: Florida State University Press, 1989), 159, emphasis added.

13. Ibid., 173.

14. Bryan Turner argues this point from the perspective of sociology.

> The phenomenology of the body offered by . . . Merleau-Ponty is an individualistic account of embodiment from the point of view of the subject; it is consequently an account largely devoid of historical and sociological content. From a sociological point of view, "the body" is socially constructed and socially experienced.

See Turner, *The Body and Society: Explorations in Social Theory* (New York: Basil Blackwell, 1984), 54.

15. See Robert Bernasconi, "Fundamental Ontology, Metontology, and the Ethics of Ethics," *Irish Philosophical Journal* 4 (1987): 76–93.

16. However, it is important to note, as Bernasconi does, that one must be cautious about reading too much into the word "metontology," because it never made its way into Heidegger's published writings. Ibid., 83.

17. See Karin de Boer, *Thinking in the Light of Time: Heidegger's Encounter with Hegel* (Albany: State University of New York Press, 2000), 12–13.

18. Heidegger goes so far as to say that "in their unity, fundamental ontology and metontology constitute the concept of metaphysics" (MFL, 158).

19. This reexamination is "decisive," as William McNeill suggests, in opening up the possibility of renewed meditations on the political and ethical nature of Dasein insofar as these domains involve analyses of the concrete comportment of human beings. See McNeill, "Metaphysics, Fundamental Ontology, and Metontology 1925–35," *Heidegger Studies* 8 (1992): 63–79. Heidegger confirms this point by saying it is only in the *existentiell* domain of metontology where "the question of an ethics may properly be raised for the first time" (MFL, 157).

Chapter 3

1. The feminist appropriation of Heidegger is particularly evident in eco-feminist theory. Consider, for instance, Carol Bigwood, *Earth Muse: Feminism, Nature, and Art* (Philadelphia, PA: Temple University Press, 1993); Trish Glazerbrook, *Heidegger's Philosophy of Science* (New York: Fordham University Press, 2000), "Heidegger and Experiment," *Philosophy Today* 42 (1998): 250–61, and "From *Physis* to Nature, *Technē* to Technology: Heidegger on Aristotle, Galileo, and Newton," *Southern Journal of Philosophy* 38 (2000): 95–118; Michael Zimmerman, *Heidegger's Confrontation with Modernity: Technology, Politics, and Art* (Bloomington: Indiana University Press, 1990), and "Feminism, Deep Ecology, and Environmental Ethics," *Environmental Ethics* 9:1 (1993): 199–224.

2. It is generally accepted that Sandra Lee Bartky's essay, "Originative Thinking in the Later Philosophy of Heidegger," published in 1970, was the

first to discuss possible affinities between Heidegger's philosophy and feminist theory. In this article, Bartky criticizes the lack of social and bodily concreteness in Heidegger's comments on overcoming technology and metaphysics in his later writings. She argues, "[Heidegger's] notion of originative thought is far too vacuous and abstract to serve the needs of any radical world-renewing project." See "Originative Thinking in the Later Philosophy of Heidegger," *Philosophy and Phenomenological Research* 30 (1970): 368.

3. Although pinning down the precise event in feminist thought or acknowledging the breadth of feminist interpretations of Heidegger over the last thirty years is beyond the scope of this project, I generally agree with Patricia Huntington, who argues that the reception of Heidegger in contemporary feminist theory came about indirectly, primarily through the influence that Jacques Derrida and Luce Irigaray had on American universities. See Huntington, "Introduction I—General Background: History of the Feminist Reception and Guide to Heidegger's Thought," in *Feminist Interpretations of Martin Heidegger*, 1–42.

4. Gayle Rubin, "The Traffic in Women: Notes on the 'Political Economy' of Sex," in *Pleasure and Danger: Exploring Female Sexuality*, ed. Carole S. Vance, 267–319 (Boston, MA: Routledge & Kegan Paul, 1984). See also Toril Moi, *Sex, Gender, and the Body: The Student Edition of What Is a Woman?* (New York: Oxford University Press, 2005), 23–30.

5. Thus as Toril Moi writes, "The [feminist] critique of the sex/gender distinction has two major objectives: (1) to avoid biological determinism; and (2) to develop a fully historical and non-essentialist understanding of sex." See Moi, *Sex, Gender, and the Body*, 30–31.

6. Heidegger makes it clear that the analytic of Dasein does not have to begin with the phenomenological description of *his* own factical existence. His *existentiell* understanding is not the "only way" to gain access to these structures. Heidegger does not restrict phenomenology to one starting point, and there is no reason to think that other descriptions of average everydayness would be excluded. The analysis of Dasein is, after all, ongoing; it is "only *one* way which we may take" (BT, 487).

7. Moi, *Sex, Gender, and the Body*, 208.

8. Simone de Beauvoir, *The Second Sex*, trans. H. M. Parshley (New York: Vintage Books, 1989), xxi.

9. Thus the individual activity of clearing (Dasein), understood as a verb, is correlative with the shared space of meaning (Da-sein), understood as a noun. See Dreyfus, *Being-in-the-World*, 165.

10. Young, *Throwing Like a Girl*, 153.

11. Ibid., 150.

12. Tina Chanter, *Ethics of Eros: Irigaray's Rewriting of the Philosophers* (New York: Routledge Press, 1995), 132–33.

13. Irigaray cites the historical forgetting of embodied "earthly" (female) sources of divinity in favor of disembodied "celestial" (male) sources that began with the rise of Greek philosophy, producing an ever-increasing concealment of a maternal language in the West. She writes:

The loss of the dimension of earthly inhabitance goes hand in hand with the neglect of Hestia in favor of the male gods, defined as celestial by philosophy from Plato onwards. These extraterrestrial gods would seem to have made us strangers to life on earth, which from then on has been thought of as an exile. (JTN, 19)

14. See Pierre Keller and David Weberman, "Heidegger and the Source(s) of Intelligibility," *Continental Philosophy Review* 31 (1998): 369–86.

15. Dreyfus, *Being-in-the-World*, 161.

16. Guignon, *Heidegger and the Problem of Knowledge*, 86.

17. Keller and Weberman, "Heidegger and the Source(s) of Intelligibility," 378.

18. "Care," therefore, is not a reference to personal "tribulation," "melancholy," or the "cares of life"; rather, care represents the unity of the various structures of Dasein, understood as a clearing of intelligibility (BT, 84). These structures are unified in terms of temporality. "[Temporality] is that which makes possible the being-ahead-of itself-in-already-being-involved-in, that is which makes possible the being of care" (HCT, 319–20).

19. See Heidegger (CT, 13–14; BT, 432); see also Charles Guignon's essay, "The History of Being," in *A Companion to Heidegger*, ed. Hubert Dreyfus and Mark Wrathall, 392–406 (New York: Blackwell Press, 2005).

20. See Heidegger (CT, 14).

21. John Caputo, "The Absence of Monica: Heidegger, Derrida, and Augustine's Confessions," in *Feminist Interpretations of Martin Heidegger*, 154.

22. Tina Chanter, "The Problematic Normative Assumptions of Heidegger's Ontology," in *Feminist Interpretations of Martin Heidegger*, 82.

23. Michel Haar, for example, takes issue with Heidegger for overemphasizing the pragmatic duties of the work world and neglecting basic bodily needs. He writes, "Must not these people occasionally stop . . . hammering. And only in order to eat, sleep, or bring a stop to the most humbly productive activities, of which [Heidegger's] analytic of Dasein breathes not a word, but quite simply, for example, in order to ponder a bouquet." See Haar, *The Song of the Earth*, 18–20.

24. Karl Löwith, *Martin Heidegger and European Nihilism*, trans. Gary Steiner (New York: Columbia University Press, 1995), 213.

25. Emmanuel Levinas, *Time and the Other*, trans. R. Cohen (Pittsburgh, PA: Duquesne University Press, 1987), 63.

26. Levinas, *Totality and Infinity: An Essay on Exteriority*, trans. Alphonso Lingis (Pittsburgh, PA: Duquesne University Press, 1969), 134, emphasis added.

27. As Carol Bigwood says, "[By] denying Eros, Heidegger remains bound to the body-denying, animal-denying, and elemental-denying tradition of Western metaphysics, despite his groundbreaking efforts to release ontological thinking from the tradition." See Bigwood, "Sappho: The She-Greek Heidegger Forgot," in *Feminist Interpretations of Martin Heidegger*, 170.

28. Judith Butler, "Sexual Ideology and Phenomenological Description: A Feminist Critique of Merleau-Ponty's *Phenomenology of Perception*," in *The Thinking Muse: Feminism and Modern French Philosophy*, ed. Jeffner Allen and Iris Marion Young, 86 (Bloomington: Indiana University Press, 1989).

29. See Carol Bigwood, *Earth Muse: Feminism, Nature, and Art* (Philadelphia, PA: Temple University Press, 1993), 23–38.

30. Bigwood, "Sappho: The She-Greek Heidegger Forgot," in *Feminist Interpretations*, 166.

31. Derrida's *Geschlecht* essays (I, II, and IV) were published in English in 1983, 1987, and 1993, respectively. *Geschlecht* I: "*Geschlecht*: Sexual Difference, Ontological Difference" was originally published in *Research in Phenomenology* 13 (1983): 65–83, and, most recently, in 2001 in *Feminist Interpretations of Martin Heidegger*, 53–72; "*Geschlecht* II: Heidegger's Hand," in *Deconstruction and Philosophy: The Texts of Jacques Derrida*, ed. John Sallis (Chicago, IL: University of Chicago Press, 1987); *Geschlecht* IV: "Heidegger's Ear: Philopolemology," in *Reading Heidegger: Commemorations*, ed. John Sallis (Bloomington: Indiana University Press, 1993). *Geschlecht* III, as of this writing, is still unpublished.

32. Heidegger emphasizes this point twice in *Being and Time*. "Philosophy is universal phenomenological ontology, and takes its departure from the hermeneutic of Dasein . . . the guiding-line for all philosophical inquiry at the point where it *arises* and to which it *returns*" (BT, 62, 487).

Chapter 4

1. See Hans Jonas, *The Phenomenon of Life* (New York: Delta, 1966); Karl Löwith, *Nature, History and Existentialism*, trans. Arnold Levinson (Evanston, IL: Northwestern University Press, 1965).

2. For French and Anglophone criticisms of Heidegger's treatment of animal life, see note 6 in the Introduction.

3. The exception here is William McNeill's pioneering essay, "Life beyond the Organism: Animal Being in Heidegger's Freiburg Lectures, 1929/30."

4. One of the goals of Heidegger's project, therefore, is to dismantle the "anthropological" interpretation of the human being as an organism. In "What Is Called Thinking?" Heidegger explains the problem of thinking of humans as biological beings.

In this distinction, anima means the fundamental determinate of every living being, including human beings. Man can be conceived as an organism, and has been so conceived for a long time. Man so conceived is then ranked with plants and animals, regardless of whether we assume that rank in order to show an evolution, or classify the genera of organisms in some other way.

Even when man is marked out as the rational living being, he is still seen in a way in which his character as an organism remains decisive—though biological phenomena, in the sense of animal and vegetable beings, may be subordinated to that rational and personal character of man which determines his life of the spirit. *All anthropology continues to be dominated by the idea that man is an organism.* (WCT, 148)

5. Thus being (*Sein*) is to be understood neither as *a* being (*das Seiende*) nor as a property of a being. Being is, rather, the disclosive "happening" (*Geschehen*) in which beings reveal themselves *as* the kinds of beings that they are (BT, 189).

6. See Calarco, "Heidegger's Zoontology," 25.

7. Jonas, *The Phenomenon of Life*, 106.

8. Heidegger, *Hölderlin's* "Germanium und Der Rhein," ed. S. Ziegler (Frankfurt am Main: Klostermann, 1980), 75.

9. Wilhelm Dilthey, *Pattern and Meaning in History*, trans. H. P. Rickman (New York: Harper Torchbooks), 73.

10. Wilhelm Dilthey, *Gesammelte Schriften*, vol. 19, cited in Bambach, *Heidegger, Dilthey, and the Crisis of Historicism* (Ithaca, NY: Cornell University Press, 1995), 155.

11. See John Caputo's "Heidegger's *Kampf*: The Difficulty of Life," *Graduate Faculty Philosophy Journal* 14:2; 15:1 (1991): 61–83.

12. Wilhelm Dilthey, *Gesammelte Schriften*, vol. 5, cited in Bambach, *Heidegger, Dilthey, and the Crisis of Historicism*, 233.

13. Wilhelm Dilthey, *Gesammelte Schriften*, vol. 5, cited in Guignon, *Heidegger and the Problem of Knowledge*, 56.

14. See Istvan M. Feher, "Phenomenology, Hermeneutics, *Lebensphilosophie*: Heidegger's Confrontation with Husserl, Dilthey, and Jaspers," in *Reading Heidegger from the Start: Essays in His Earliest Thought*, ed. Theodore Kisiel and John van Buren, 73–89 (Albany: State University of New York Press, 1994).

15. The phrase "secret weapon" here is borrowed from Theodore Kisiel in his essay, "Heidegger (1920–21) on Becoming a Christian: A Conceptual Picture Show," in *Reading Heidegger from the Start: Essays in His Earliest Thought*, 178.

16. Heidegger, *Phänomenologie der Anschauung und des Ausdrucks* (Frankfurt am Main: Klostermann, 1993), 85, cited in Karin de Boer, *Thinking in the Light of Time*, 88.

17. It is in coming to grips with this relational sense of human activity that Heidegger abandoned the word "life" altogether. For Heidegger, *Leben* failed to capture the unique way in which we *ek-sist* or "stand outside" of ourselves, insofar as we are always already directed toward a background of social relations. By 1923, seeking a more "rigorous" and "philosophically precise concept," Heidegger began to swear off the ambiguous word "life" for the more neutral, systematic, and technical word "Dasein." See Heidegger (HF, 24–27).

18. Michel Haar writes, "One could object that Heidegger's phenomenology has taken into account neither the cries, moaning, nor the grimaces, mimicry, gestures, and postures which are irrefutably modes of expression among, for example, mammals." See Haar, *The Song of the Earth*, 29; see also Jonas, *The Phenomenon of Life*, 106.

19. Guignon, *Heidegger and the Problem of Knowledge*, 111–12; see also Guignon, "Heidegger: Language as the House of Being," in *The Philosophy of Discourse: The Rhetorical Turn in Twentieth-Century Thought, Vol. II*, ed. Chip Sills and George H. Jensen, 171–77 (Portsmouth, NH: Boynton/Cook, 1992).

20. Clifford Geertz, *The Interpretation of Cultures* (New York: Basic Books, 1973), 50.

21. Guignon, "Heidegger: Language as the House of Being," 175.

22. Dreyfus, *Being-in-the-World*, 17.

23. McNeill, *The Time of Life: Heidegger and Ethos* (Albany: State University of New York Press, 2006), 38, 48.

24. See Krell, *Daimon Life*, 10, 181.

25. In addition to anxiety, Heidegger also acknowledges a number of other fundamental moods—including "profound boredom" (in the 1929–30 lectures), which we will explore in chapter 5, and "intense joy" (in the 1936 Nietzsche lecture "The Will to Power as Art")—that open us up to the contingency and unsettledness of being.

26. Heidegger writes, "[It] is questionable whether death [is] the same in the case of man and animal, even if we can identify a physico-chemical and physiological equivalence between the two. Is the death of the animal a dying or a way of coming to an end? Because 'captivation' belongs to the essence of the animal, the animal cannot die in the sense in which dying is ascribed to human being but can only come to an end" (FCM, 267).

27. Heidegger revisits this theme in his later lectures when he discusses what it means to be a "mortal." He explains, "The mortals are human beings. They are called mortals because they can die. To die means to be capable of death as death. Only man dies. The animal perishes" (TT, 176).

28. Here I am following Theodore Kisiel's argument in *The Genesis of Being and Time* (Berkeley: University of California Press, 1993), 21–68.

29. Theodore Kisiel, "Why Students of Heidegger Will Have to Read Emil Lask," *Man and World* 28 (1995): 227.

30. Stephen Crowell, "Lask, Heidegger, and the Homelessness of Logic," *Journal of the British Society for Phenomenology* 23 (1992): 223.

31. The influence of Emil Lask on Heidegger's project cannot be overstated. As Heinrich Rickert, the teacher of both Lask and Heidegger, says: "[Heidegger] is in particular very much obligated to Lask's writing for his philosophical orientation as well as his terminology, perhaps more than he himself is conscious of." Cited in Kisiel, *The Genesis of* Being and Time, 25. See also Crowell, "Lask, Heidegger, and the Homelessness of Logic," 222–39; István M. Fehér, "Lask, Lukacs, Heidegger: The Problem of Irrationality and the Theory of Categories," in *Martin Heidegger: Critical Assessments, Vol. II: History of Philosophy*, ed. Christopher Macann, 373–405 (New York: Routledge,

1992); Michael Friedman, *Parting of the Ways: Carnap, Cassirer, and Heidegger* (Chicago, IL: Open Court Press, 2000), 35–36, 39–41; Kisiel, "Why Students of Heidegger Will Have to Read Emil Lask," 197–240.

32. Here I am particularly indebted to Crowell's article, "Lask, Heidegger, and the Homelessness of Logic," 226–27.

33. Kisiel, "Why Students of Heidegger Will Have to Read Emil Lask," 199.

34. Joseph Campbell, *The Power of Myth* (New York: Doubleday, 1988), 34.

35. McNeill, *The Time of Life*, xii.

36. See Franois Raffoul, *Heidegger and the Subject,* trans. David Pettigrew and Gregory Recco (Amherst, NY: Humanities Books, 1999), 161–65.

37. See Daniela Vallega-Neu, *The Bodily Dimension in Thinking* (Albany: State University of New York Press, 2005), 83–102.

38. Vallega-Neu, *Heidegger's Contribution to Philosophy* (Bloomington: Indiana University Press, 2003), 9.

39. Ibid., 25.

40. Ibid., 28.

Chapter 5

1. Tom Lutz, *American Nervousness, 1903: An Anecdotal History* (Ithaca, NY: Cornell University Press, 1991), 4. See also Michael O' Malley, "The Busyness That Is Not Business: Nervousness and Character at the Turn of the Century," *Social Research* 72:2 (2005): 371–406.

2. Cited in Diane Ulmer and Leonard Schwartzburd, *Heart and Mind: The Practice of Cardiac Psychology* (Washington, DC: American Psychological Association, 1996), 329.

3. Besides "Echo," Heidegger lists "Playing-Forth," "Leap," "Grounding," "The Ones to Come," and "The Last God" as the other fugues. These fugues are not to be understood as progressive or chronologically ordered but as repetitions of the same movement of history or "be-ing," which Heidegger refers to with the eighteenth-century orthography *Seyn*.

> In each of the six joining the attempt is made always to say the same [*das Selbe*] of the same, but in each case from within another essential domain of that which enowning names. Seen externally and fragmentarily, one easily finds "repetitions" everywhere. But what is most difficult is purely to enact in accord with the jointure, a persevering with the same, this witness of genuine inabiding of inceptual thinking. (CP, 57)

4. Karl Marx, "Manifesto of the Communist Party," in *The Marx-Engels Reader*, ed. Robert Tucker, 469–500 (New York: W. W. Norton, 1978).

5. Weber, *The Protestant Ethic and the Spirit of Capitalism*, trans. Talcott Parsons (Los Angeles: Roxbury, 1998), 157–58.

6. Emile Durkheim, *Suicide: A Study in Sociology*, trans. John A. Spaulding and George Simpson (New York: The Free Press, 1979).

7. Robert Levine, *A Geography of Time* (New York: Basic Books, 1997), 20–21.

8. As we saw in chapter 1, Heidegger dismantles the ordinary interpretation of time—understood as a linear "process" (*Vorgang*) or sequence of "nows" that can be measured and organized by clocks and calendars into hours, days, weeks, and years. For Heidegger, everyday "clock time" is itself made possible by "primordial time," understood as an interconnected manifold of the "ecstatic" structures of "past" (*Gewesenheit*), "present" (*Gegenwart*) and "future" (*Zukunft*). These structures represent the a priori scaffolding or frame of reference on the basis of which things can show up *as* the very things that they are.

9. Kenneth Gergen, *The Saturated Self: Dilemmas of Identity in Contemporary Life* (New York: Basic Books, 1991).

10. These points are taken from David Cerbone's essay, "Heidegger and Dasein's Bodily Nature," 218–19.

11. Hans-Georg Gadamer, *The Enigma of Health: The Art of Healing in the Scientific Age*, trans. Jason Gaiger and Nicholas Walker (Stanford, CA: Stanford University Press, 1996), 112.

12. Ibid., 113–14.

13. See Aho, "Simmel on Acceleration, Boredom, and Extreme Aesthesia," *Journal for the Theory of Social Behavior* 37:4 (2007): 445–60, esp. 450–51.

14. Ulmer and Schwartzburd, *Heart and Mind*, 331–32. According to Ulmer and Schwartzburd, hurry sickness can be diagnosed if the subject suffers from, among other things: (1) "deterioration of the personality, marked primarily by loss of interest in aspects of life except those connected with achievement of goals and by a preoccupation with numbers, with a growing tendency to evaluate life in terms of quantity rather than quality," (2) "racing mind syndrome, characterized by rapid, shifting thoughts that gradually erode the ability to focus and concentrate and create disruption of sleep," (3) "loss of ability to accumulate pleasant memories, mainly due to either preoccupation with future events or rumination about past events, with little attention to the present."

15. Ibid., 332.

16. Georg Simmel, "The Metropolis and Mental Life," in *Simmel on Culture*, ed. David Frisby and Mike Featherstone, 179 (London: Sage Publications, 1997).

17. Ibid., 176.

18. Ibid.

19. Ibid., 178.

20. Ibid., 179.

21. Ibid.

22. Ibid., 184.

23. This course expands on Heidegger's inaugural Freiburg lecture, given on July 24, 1929, entitled "What Is Metaphysics?" In this lecture, the mood of boredom is explored for the first time.

24. Here I am indebted to Parvis Emad's essay, "Boredom as Limit and Disposition," *Heidegger Studies* 64:1 (1985): 63–78.

25. To this end, the German word for boredom captures something that the French or English renditions cannot. *Langeweile* is literally the unpleasant mood that accompanies an empty stretch of time; it is "the lengthening and lingering of the while (*Weile*)." See Emad, "Boredom as Limit and Disposition," 67.

26. Dreyfus, *Being-in-the-World*, 168.

27. Philip Cushman, "Why the Self Is Empty: Toward a Historically Situated Psychology," *American Psychologist* 45:5 (1990): 601.

28. Heidegger, "Messkirch Seventh Centennial," trans. Thomas Sheehan, *Listening* 8:1 (1973): 50–51.

29. Cushman, "Why the Self Is Empty," 606.

30. Ludwig Binswanger, "Existential Analysis and Psychotherapy," in *Progress In Psychotherapy*, ed. Frieda Fromm-Reichmann and J. L. Moreno, 145 (New York: Grune and Stratton, 1956).

31. Bertrand Russell, *Our Knowledge of the External World* (New York: Mentor Books, 1956), 142. See also Kenneth Gergen, "Social Psychology as History," *Journal of Personality and Social Psychology* 26:2 (1973): 309–20, esp. 309.

32. Thomas Nagel, *Moral Questions* (New York: Cambridge University Press, 1979), 208.

33. Martin Seligman and Mihaly Csikszentmihalyi, "Positive Psychology: An Introduction," *American Psychologist* 55:1 (2000): 5.

34. Sigmund Freud, *Standard Edition of the Complete Psychological Works of Sigmund Freud* (London: Hogarth Press, 1964), 171. See also Richard Askey, "Heidegger's Philosophy and Its Implications for Psychology, Freud, and Existential Psychoanalysis," in Heidegger, *Zollikon Seminars*, 309.

35. Cushman, "Why the Self Is Empty," 599–611.

36. Ibid., 609.

37. For instance, the journal *American Psychologist* recently devoted an entire volume to the resurgent movement of positive psychology. See *American Psychologist* 55:1 (2000).

38. Seligman and Csikszentmihalyi, "Positive Psychology: An Introduction," 6.

39. Guignon, "Hermeneutics, Authenticity, and the Aims of Psychology," *Journal of Theoretical and Philosophical Psychology* 22 (2002): 86.

40. Seligman and Csikszentmihalyi, "Positive Psychology: An Introduction," 8.

41. Guignon, "Hermeneutics, Authenticity, and the Aims of Psychology," 88.

42. See Barry Schwartz, "Self-Determination: The Tyranny of Freedom," *American Psychologist* 55:1 (2000): 79–88.

43. See George Vaillant, "Adaptive Mental Mechanisms: Their Role in Positive Psychology," *American Psychologist* 55:1 (2000): 89–98.

44. See Dean Keith Simonton, "Creativity, Cognitive, Personal, Developmental, and Social," *American Psychologist* 55:1 (2000): 151–58.

45. See David Buss, "The Evolution of Happiness," *American Psychologist* 55:1 (2000): 15–23.

Chapter 6

1. Thomas C. Anderson, "Technology and the Decline of Leisure," *Proceedings of the American Catholic Philosophical Association* 70 (1997): 1.

2. Hans Jonas, "Heidegger's *Entschlossenheit und Entschluss*," in *Antwort: Martin Heidegger im Gespräch*, ed. G. Neske and E. Kettering, 226–27 (Pfullingen: G. Neske Verlag, 1988), cited in Richard Wolin, "Karl Löwith and Martin Heidegger—Contexts and Controversies: An Introduction," in Karl Löwith, *Martin Heidegger and European Nihilism*, trans. Gary Steiner, 8 (New York: Columbia University Press, 1995). The criticism of Heidegger's "decisionism" has been taken up more recently by Jürgen Habermas, in *The Philosophical Discourse of Modernity: Twelve Lectures*, trans. Frederick G. Lawrence (Cambridge, MA: MIT Press, 1987), and Richard Wolin, in *The Politics of Being: The Political Thought of Martin Heidegger* (New York: Columbia University Press, 1990).

3. It is for this reason that Heidegger writes, "Inauthentic historicality lies in the title of 'everydayness' " (BT, 428).

4. See Guignon, "Heidegger's 'Authenticity' Revisited," *Review of Metaphysics* 38 (1984): 321–39.

5. Joan Stambaugh, "Heidegger, Taoism, and Metaphysics," in *Heidegger and Asian Thought*, ed. Graham Parkes, 86 (Honolulu: University of Hawaii Press, 1987).

6. Although they were contemporaries in Germany, I have discovered no evidence of a correspondence between Heidegger and Pieper.

7. Josef Pieper, *In Tune with the World: A Theory of Festivity*, trans. Richard and Clara Winston (Chicago, IL: Franciscan Herald Press, 1965), 2.

8. Josef Pieper, *Leisure as the Basis of Culture*, trans. Alexander Dru (New York: Random House, 1963), 70.

9. It is important to note that the English word for leisure comes from the Latin *licere* ("to be allowed"), which implies a freedom from restraint. See Joseph Owens, "Aristotle on Leisure," *Canadian Journal of Philosophy* 11:4 (1981): 715.

10. Pieper, *Leisure as the Basis of Culture*, 21.

11. Ibid., 21.

12. Ibid., 20. See also Aristotle, *Politics,* 13334a11, in *Aristotle Selections*, trans. Terence Irwin and Gail Fine (Indianapolis, IN: Hackett, 1995), 515.

Aristotle's most detailed discussion of leisure is in the *Politics*, 1333a30–b5; 1334a11–40; 1337b29–1338a30; Owens, "Aristotle on Leisure," 715.

13. Pieper, *Leisure as the Basis of Culture*, 38.

14. Ibid., 40.

15. Ibid.

16. Ibid., 43.

17. Describing festivity, Pieper writes, "I am referring to the concept of play. Does not play epitomize that pure purposefulness in itself, we might ask? Is not play activity meaningful in itself, needing no utilitarian justification? And should not festivity therefore be interpreted chiefly as a form of play?" See Pieper, *In Tune with the World*, 8.

18. Eugen Fink, "The Ontology of Play," *Philosophy Today* 4 (1960): 98.

19. Ibid., 101.

20. In his *Contributions to Philosophy*, Heidegger identifies "playing forth" (*zuspiel*) as "preparation for the other beginning," a new epoch that retrieves the hidden sources of the "first beginning" of Greek thinkers who experienced truth (*a-lethia*) in terms of the unconcealment of beings (CP, 12).

21. Fink, "The Ontology of Play," 106.

22. Hans-Georg Gadamer, *Truth and Method*, trans. Joel Weinsheimer and Donald G. Marshall (New York: Continuum Press, 1994), 106.

23. See Julian Young, *Heidegger's Later Philosophy* (New York: Cambridge University Press, 2000), 58.

24. Martin Heidegger, *Gesamtausgabe 52*, "Holderlin's Hymn '*Andenken*,' " ed. F.-W. von Herrmann, 64 (Frankfurt am Main: Klostermann, 1977), cited in Young, *Heidegger's Later Philosophy*, 60.

25. Heidegger, "Phenomenological Interpretations in Connection with Aristotle: An Indication of the Hermeneutic Situation," in *Supplements: From the Earliest Essays to* Being and Time *and Beyond*, trans. John van Buren, 114 (Albany: State University of New York Press, 2002). See also Charles Guignon, "Philosophy and Authenticity: Heidegger's Search for a Ground for Philosophizing," in *Heidegger, Authenticity, and Modernity: Essays in Honor of Hubert L. Dreyfus, Volume I*, ed. Mark A. Wrathall and Jeff Malpas, 95–97 (Cambridge: MIT Press, 2000).

26. Hubert Dreyfus draws our attention to this overlooked passage in his essay "Nihilism, Art, Technology, and Politics," in *The Cambridge Companion to Heidegger*, ed. Guignon, 345–72.

27. Here I am indebted to Julian Young's analysis in *Heidegger's Later Philosophy*, 122–27.

28. Nietzsche, "Sils Maria," cited in Stambaugh, "Heidegger, Taoism, and Metaphysics," 86.

29. "*Der Speigel* Interview," in *Martin Heidegger and National Socialism*, ed. Gunther Neske and Emil Kettering, 41–66 (New York: Paragon House, 1990).

30. See Wolin, *The Politics of Being*, 151; Young, *Heidegger's Later Philosophy*, 84.

31. Young, *Heidegger's Later Philosophy*, 88.

32. Thich Nhat Hanh, *The Heart of Understanding* (Berkeley, CA: Parallax Press, 1988), 3–5.

33. Gail Stenstad, *Transformations: Thinking after Heidegger* (Madison: University of Wisconsin Press, 2006), 90. I am especially indebted to Stenstad for her reading of the later Heidegger.

34. Albert Hofstadter translates *Schonen* as "sparing and preserving." I am following Julian Young's rendering of the word as "caring-for." See Young, *Heidegger's Later Philosophy*, 64, n. 2.

35. Young, "The Fourfold," in *The Cambridge Companion to Heidegger*, ed. Guignon, 388.

Index

acceleration (*Beschleunigung*), 5,
105, 107–108, 114, 149. *See*
technology
acedia, 135. *See* boredom
Agamben, Giorgio, 151n.6
alienation, 123
ambiguity (*Zweideutigkeit*), 128–129
Anderson, Thomas, 165n.1
animal, rational, 74–75, 87
anomie, 108, 123. *See* Durkheim,
Emil
anxiety (*Angst*), 5, 63–64, 95, 101,
123, 129, 131, 161n.25. *See* Dasein
anyone. *See* the They (*das Man*)
Aristotle, 8, 79, 122, 133; on leisure,
134, 165–166n.12; *Nicomachean
Ethics*, 122; *Politics*, 133
Askay, Richard, 151n.1, 154n.1,
164n.34
authenticity (*Eigentlichkeit*). *See*
Dasein, Heidegger, temporality
(*Zeitlichkeit*)

Bartky, Sandra Lee, 156–157n.2
Beard, George, 105
Beauvoir, Simone de, 56, 157n.8
be-ing-historical thinking
(*seynsgeschichtliches Denken*), 102
being (*Sein*): meaning of, 1, 4, 6,
16–17, 70, 102–103; mystery of, 6,
124, 149; of beings (*Seiendes*), 7–8,
17, 54, 98, 102, 106, 160n.5
beings (*Seiendes*), 7–8, 17, 54, 96,
98, 102, 106, 115, 125, 160n.5;
enchantment with, 117–118,

129, 134, 138; gathering of, 136,
144–145
Being and Time. *See* Heidegger
being-in-the-world (*In-der-Welt-sein*).
See Dasein
being-towards-the-beginning, 132
being-towards-death, 128–129
behavior (*Benehmen*), 2–3, 73, 76–77
Bergson, Henri, 79
Bernasconi, Robert, 156n.16
Bigwood, Carol, 67, 156n.1, 158n.27,
159n.29–30
Binswanger, Ludwig, 118, 164n.30
blasé attitude. *See* Simmel
body. *See*, corporeal body (*Körper*),
Dasein, lived-body (*Leib*)
Boer, Karin de, 156n.17, 160n.16
boredom (*Langeweile*), 5, 101,
113–116, 119, 134, 164n.23;
becoming bored by something
(*Gelangweiltwerden von etwas*),
114; being bored with something
(*Sichlangweilen bei etwas*), as
conspicuous, 114–115; ennui, 117;
as inconspicuous, 115–117, 134;
114–115, 123; profound boredom
(*tiefe Langeweile*), 5, 115, 161n.25
Boss, Medard, 29, 118
Bourdieu, Pierre, 32, 41, 155n.9
Buss, David, 165n.45
Butler, Judith, 66, 159n.28

Calarco, Matthew, 73, 152n.6, 160n.6
calculation, 105, 107, 149. *See*
technological age

Made in the USA
Middletown, DE
14 June 2022